Many Dwelling Places

Many Dwelling Places

Discovering Your True Purpose in Life

CHARLES LEHN

ISBN: 979-8-218-94782-8

Disclaimer

This book is proposed to offer spiritual guidance and insight for personal reflection. The content is based on Catholic teaching and provides information for those seeking to deepen their faith and consider purpose for their lives. The author does not provide medical, psychological, or legal advice. Please consult professionals in those fields as necessary. The concepts and information expressed in this book are for personal development and should not be a substitute for religious or spiritual direction from your faith director.

"Do not let your hearts be troubled. Believe in God, believe also in me. In my Father's house there are many dwelling-places. If that were not so, would I have told you that I go to prepare a place for you? And if I go and prepare a place for you, I will come again and will take you to myself so that where I am, there you may be also. Thomas said to him, 'Lord, we do not know where you are going. How can we know the way?' Jesus said to him, 'I am the Way, and the Truth, and the Life. No one comes to the Father except through me.'"

(John 14 1-6)

THIS BOOK IS WRITTEN to express my infinite gratitude to God for sending His only Son to save me a super sinner, especially when He did not have to do so.

The book's purpose is to point people to Jesus and assist in saving their souls in this life and the next by helping them discover their purpose in life and their heavenly dwelling place.

The book is dedicated to my wife Nicky for helping me grasp the gift of God's great love and sacrifice.

To my parents for enduring and persevering in their marriage in a time where divorce was an easy option.

It is with thanksgiving to and in the spirit of St. Sr. Faustina Kowalska's trust in Jesus, and for her intercession that this book realizes final print.

It is because of St. Faustina that I can say:

Jesus, I Trust in YOU!

St. Francis De Sales, patron Saint of writers, I pray that you intercede these words spotlight Jesus.

Thank you to Anonymous for your editing! You made me consider what Jesus would want said.

Finally, I could not have written this book without the help of the Blessed Mother's guidance and intercession. I have learned that wherever Jesus is, you will find His Holy Mother there too.

It is the intent that this book assist souls find their purpose by learning that Jesus Christ is the Way the Truth and the Life to their Heavenly Dwelling Place, the Father's House.

"Jesus and Mary, I love you Save souls!"

(This 'Act of Love' includes all souls, the souls in purgatory, the innocent, the suffering, the sinful, the dying and even your own poor soul. Do not lose time! Every 'Act of Love' means a soul. … and repairs a thousand blasphemies! Words of Our Lord to Sr. Maria Consolata Betrone, Poor Clare Capuchin (1930-1946). Imprimatur: +M. Cardinal Fossati, Archbishop of Turin, Italy, October 1, 1949. Pieta Prayer Booklet, Pg. 20

TABLE OF CONTENTS

FOREWORD

Keeping an open mind and heart will help you find your purpose.

What would motivate you to want to read this book on discovering one's purpose in life? There are so many books written and available today, some good and informative, some more entertaining than anything. This book serves to help readers acknowledge their one purpose, their final resting place amidst a world that can be cruel and unforgiving, and at other times one that begs the question, "What is my purpose in this life"? I am hoping the title and subtitle catch your attention, because this book deals with the most important question in life. Better yet, this writing helps remind the reader that God is calling you to focus on your eternal future with Him.

This writing is produced to bring real and authentic hope and joyfulness, while encouraging one to not give up in their daily trials and tests. When is the last time you had true childlike hope in something? This book will present facts and quotes, through examples, small stories, and scriptural references. These are meant to plainly give one hesitation and pause to consider all things. Not in so much a philosophical fashion, but rather genuine reality and day to day living. Do yourself a huge favor and read this with an open mind. If you apply these aspects to your new mindset, you will have a new outlook on your purpose in life. There is nothing to lose reading this book, but rather it focuses on your future and making investments that will reward in this life and the next.

Encouragement and little discoveries will foster your determination.

This book is written to bring you the tangible and intangible you did not know or consider regarding the trials and tribulations encountered in life. Its purpose is to encourage you to follow the examples of Jesus Christ to set you towards heaven (the Father's House). Your ultimate dwelling place.

Following the examples and instructions of Jesus Christ, and what is to be understood as parable or literal meaning helps achieve this end. Developing virtues that produce bona fide good is key to creating our foundation and following our Lord's example. Through this process of developing good, one puts bits and pieces together regarding the special and unique circumstances in your life and how they must fit some sort of high-level plan. As time goes on you discover that you are part of a bigger organized design. You come to the realization that you were meant to love, know and serve the one true God, and that He loves you beyond human comprehension. This book helps you come to this realization.

It is anticipated that the reader will discover tremendous hopefulness, peace, and a purposeful resolve when completed with the reading. Maybe you already have some knowledge of what is presented, but the book is written to provide encouragement, enrichment, basic understandings, and to visualize an overall purpose in living this gift of life.

It is requested that you have an open heart, and open mind, and to ask God to reveal the truth in your conscience while reading this piece. What is truth you might ask? A wise old 1952 Emmy award winning Bishop from the 1950's, Archbishop Fulton J. Sheen once said, *"Truth is the truth even if no one believes it, and a lie is a lie even if everyone believes it".* Jesus and His Church is certainly truth. It would not have lasted two-thousand plus years if it was not. It is this author's promise not to refer you to anything false, but to point to that truth. It is encouraged as you read that you verify what is presented by your own heart's conviction. Your conscience will not fail you to know if what is being stated is true or not. It is my heartfelt attempt that all things presented are true in this writing.

It is hoped that you request that God our Father reveal to you Jesus Christ in some way, shape, or form. This is His son whom He sent to rescue us from evil. Ultimately it is asked of the reader to believe Jesus to be that truth for your life, by letting your defenses down for a moment and soaking in what is being presented. Please be open and you will understand why later! Jesus will take over if you invite Him into your life. You just need to be serious and sincerely reach out and ask for His help.

Before one undertakes anything in this life, it is wise to pray to God for His assistance to help you with what you need. Reading this writing is no different. Let us pray this brief and direct prayer to help you slowly soak in what is presented, and to let it touch your heart and mind where there might be confusion, doubt, despair, hurt or anger. These negative things are not from God. So, we ask the opposite! *"Dear Lord Jesus Christ, we ask that you cover us with your most precious blood that you shed by embracing the cross. We ask you for You to protect our minds, open our hearts, and convict in us your truth as we read this writing. We ask you to bless us with knowledge and wisdom, and help us to do your will after reading this text. All this we ask by your Holy and Mighty name Jesus!"*

Getting through this life and its arduous daily challenges can sap and deplete us of our energy and motivation for living. We truly need examples of superhuman strength, perseverance, and endurance to provide us revitalizing reassurance and the ability to go forward each day. While we may arguably live in one of the most difficult centuries since the beginning of man with its insane levels of stress, confusion, and darkness, our God provides us an example in Himself and other highly resilient people and their stories. He sends us much needed grace to overcome the wickedness that is working against us nonstop. We continue our existence in search of purpose and reaffirmation that we indeed matter and are loved. It is our responsibility to at least try and understand our purpose. That purpose without hesitation is to dwell with our Lord after our earthly lives and obtain the great reward He has for being faithful.

Fortunately, there are many examples and stories of others that can inspire us to get up each day and undertake the burdens that life deals us. We will consider some of these stories later in the writing. While we often possess these innate and sturdy inner qualities of strength, perseverance and endurance at our core, each of us exhibit these distinctively and at various levels of effectiveness. It is the ability to utilize these virtues and harness the motivation necessary to bear the weight and afflictions that subdue us and overwhelm us in our earthly lives and daily duties.

It is the author's desire that people be able to overcome, have life to the fullest, and be most joyous in their existence! It is often the case that people have others counting on them to withstand challenging circumstances and to be functional after hard times cease. Parents need to be there for their kids, spouses should be there for each other, adults ought to be there to support elderly parents, friends must be true life savers to other friends (true friends as the book of Sirach talks about 6: 14-17), "*Beyond price, no amount can balance their worth*". Relatives and families are required to support one another despite being in a "less than harmonious" relationship. The purpose of this book is to help those brothers and sisters reading this who are fatigued to the point where they believe (or who are starting to wane in belief) that their troubles and problems are too immeasurable to handle.

The writing's purpose is to highlight and give evidence that the place where Jesus wants our final destination to be is heaven! This book provides examples of Jesus's interactions and instructions. It points out how He is "the Way" to what He describes as "many dwelling places" in His Father's house.

For those afflicted with a mindset that they cannot "keep on keeping on" with the crushing oppressions that different seasons in our lives deliver, this book is for you. This book is for encouragement to focus on this ultimate destination. To find purpose in wanting to live happily with our Lord in paradise once this earthly test is done is what this writing is all about.

Examples are furnished of others whose earthly difficulties, hardships, and sufferings were overcome by a high display of these virtues and faith in God. Our main character in these examples is our Lord Jesus Christ. These stories also demonstrate that through strength, perseverance, and endurance, one can overcome these "tests" and reach down deep and access those superhuman features when necessary.

By accessing and applying these inner virtues, one sets their face like flint as our Lord did on the cross. Jesus makes evident His resolve that He came to provide us a door to eternity. These stories have in common that God's providence and grace supply for us in our lives. The reader is to learn that prayer and trust in Him who is Trustworthiness and Mercy itself, namely Jesus Christ, bring about victory and peace. Faith in Him and doing His will carries the day at the end of our lives. We find ourselves heading to heaven.

Certain situations will challenge the very composition of our physical, mental and spiritual personhood at some point in our lives. These phases and states of complications will sometimes be for short periods of time, and others for longer durations. The final goal for all of us is to find purpose in our lives so that we can achieve not only joy and happiness here, but ultimately heaven. This writing takes the reader in that direction. Heaven is the goal and that is why it is imperative to find purpose in this life.

Every day is a new opportunity to learn and overcome.

The writing covers a multitude of topics that culminate to provide information and examples of why it is important not to despair, worry, become dejected, demoralized. These topics, on the contrary, are poised and presented to build oneself up by providing considerations, examples, and things you may have not thought about until now. Learning and applying these considerations will lead you to that purpose that has significant meaning and the desire to continue.

Everyone enjoys stories and examples, and these help us along our way. However, this book also uncovers the ultimate source of strength, perseverance and endurance in Jesus Christ. For those of you who may not know Him, He is the Way, the Truth and the Life for all things. He tells us this in the 14th Chapter in St. John's Gospel. He is your everything! It is recommended that you have a bible by your side when you read to reference some of the important biblical references. Not just any bible, but a Catholic Bible that has not had is words refined, and the meaning altered in any way. This is significantly important to understand, that many Protestant versions of the bible do not provide the original text nor their meanings. This is not a knock towards Protestantism, (because they once had what they refer to as the "apocrypha"), but there were seven books removed during the Reformation. This is a simple fact from history. From there many Protestant bibles translated things and omitted certain aspects and were simply altered. This author recommends the New Revised Standard Version Catholic Edition Holy Bible.

It is sufficient that the reader knows that this book will help bare the facts, that, when you rely and call on Him, Jesus Christ, to get through any difficulty, He will come to your assistance. This reading will disclose the simple ways to call out to Him for these virtues. The reading will also direct you to draw on His Holy Love and Mercy, because He wants to understand that everyone needs to rely on Him for all things.

Another request of those reading this book is to keep an open mind and heart regarding the concepts of Christianity, namely Catholic Christianity. While demonstrating examples and explaining the value of certain notions and views, the author provides the reasons why certain beliefs held are of immense worth and meaning. Sometimes, simply because of pride and arrogance, or the fact that the evil one does not want you to know something, one will willfully and intentionally shuffle by a particular thought and consideration. One will be given the thought that a certain idea is foolishness or false. When that happens, resist that temptation and ask your guardian angel and the Holy Spirit to enlighten you regarding the topic. (Yes! You have a guardian angel and that angel is a manifest gift from God to be loved and respected for their role in getting you to the dwelling place!). While angels are another topic for another study, our souls would be much more in jeopardy had we not been given each a guardian angel. Our guardian angels point us in the direction of our heavenly dwelling place. *"Take care that you do not despise one of these little ones; for I tell you, in heaven their angels continually see the face of my Father in heaven" (Matthew 18: 10-11).*

Do not listen to bad information, the Church was created specifically for you.

Forget whatever poor advice or negative reference you have had of the Catholic Church. The Catholic Church, while not perfect, is the one true Church that Jesus founded. It can name its leadership all the way back, pope by pope, to St. Peter. Jesus gave His apostles direction to spread the Gospel everywhere and to do it in His Name. Jesus is the Way the Truth and the Life. This is not a book whose main focus is to convert one to the Catholic faith. However, because of many truths, the Catholic faith is indeed highlighted in this reading, because the text is about truth and finding one's purpose.

People need to find their purpose in life. They need to find God and lean on Him. People are led away all the time. They can have different missions and still have one purpose. They are led away from the one thing that will solve all issues and remove all pain. That thing that they are led away from is a relationship with Jesus.

This writing is one resource that points anyone who reads it in the proper direction. That direction is towards your heavenly home. There is only one way to get there and that is Jesus. The pathway to Jesus includes the sacraments He provides for us in His Church. It is the way He set things up and the way the Holy Spirit becomes active in our lives. Hopefully the reader will make the connection that the Holy Mother Church, a reference to the Catholic Church, was made for you and me.

The Truth will be your greatest ally.

It is imperative for you to cultivate and ask for the Holy Spirit, Jesus's Spirit, to make known to you many truths. The enemy, the devil, will try all trickery, and falsehoods, and deception to lead you away from Jesus and His Church. All that is presented in this book is truth. Jesus Christ is the Truth. There is no other spin or rationale in this reading other than to point the reader to heaven. This book is written so the reader understand they are in the middle of the "test".

Jesus will not let you be led astray if you continue to ask Him to show you this truth. The premises and conclusions presented in this writing are basic and simple. Things are repeated at the risk of tedium, but drive home concepts for those who need to hear things a number of times for things to sink in. All points made lead back to the Lamb of God. The Sovereign King who is in love with us and wants that relationship if you, the reader, will allow it. He does not force us ever to accept Him. This is our choice and the most important choice you will ever make. Do not follow the secondary thoughts that the evil one wants you to believe. He, the devil, wants you not to believe and uses negative and false information to lead you away from Jesus. Do not fall for this, the oldest deception in history. He knows Jesus is King. He, the devil, also keenly knows his time to act against our souls is short.

The reader is asked to be deliberate in their reflection on these beliefs and humble themselves while contemplating on and imitating what you are provided for examples. It is very hard to humble oneself in the world we live in. However, by submitting to and achieving humility, (in essence surrendering to humility) you are equipped to address all life's challenges and perspectives. It is then that God lavishes on His grace, help and love. We will also study a handful of other virtues that make the ability to utilize strength, perseverance, and endurance in the right way very applicable and necessary.

Self-Awareness

The manuscript is presented with the understanding that there will be a variety of levels of awareness of the Holy Bible or scripture, and these references are made to provide credence to what is being explained. While not overbearing, in all transparency, the text has an underlying Roman Catholic instructional that tries to reach various levels that people might be at in their spiritual continuum/ setting. All things presented here again are truth and meant solely to get the reader closer to what matters most; that of being with and residing one day with God.

PREFACE

Doing something to repay God for His goodness

Have you ever had a compelling, ongoing, nudge to do something significant for the Lord who created you? Each person has unique attributes and gifts. To discover these and form them to assist self and others is part of what life is all about. This book is about finding purpose and meaning by studying the examples of strength, perseverance, and endurance and other virtues. It is about recognizing these virtues in others to inspire us to continue "fighting the good fight" each day and practice them ourselves.

One concept that is integral in finding purpose is putting into perspective what it means for all humans to be part of a mystical unit of togetherness after a physical and spiritual Baptism in Jesus Christ. Have you ever heard this analogy regarding being "members" or "parts" of the body of Christ? Have you wondered what purpose you individually may contribute to this body? " While the concept is described as an analogy in Holy scripture, Holy scripture also reveals that it is actually true when you understand yourself to be members of the body of Christ. This means we all contribute as members to this body. *"Now you are the body of Christ and individually members of it"* (1 Corinthians: 27). These members produce physical, mental, and spiritual properties to this body and this book will help you uncover some of your own personal contributions to this body. This body is ultimately destined to end up in heaven, the dwelling place that is our ultimate destiny. One also has to remember that we have an obligation to assist one another to get to this place. It is part of finding our purpose, and this purpose can have various facets that all point us to getting to Jesus's Father's House.

The idea is that we all contribute to the betterment of one another and that each person has significance. Being members in this body then, one can begin to understand one's own vital significance and worth. If you are not yet a member of this body, but feel compelled and called to be part of this heavenly membership after reading this book, I will point you in the direction for the next steps to take in your journey. It means becoming full-fledged participants in this mysterious yet fully alive and vibrant unit for God.

As part of this concept of being members of Christ's body there is another aspect that is so crucial to understanding one's significance. The importance of knowing that we are temples of the Holy Spirit. To back up for a moment, one needs to understand that the God we serve is three separate persons. Each person of the Trinity, God the Father, God the Son, and God the Holy Spirit, are also God "*whole and entire*" (Catechism of the Catholic Church, 253). and are referred to as the Holy Trinity. For those who are familiar with the reality of the Holy Trinity, that of the Father, the Son (Jesus Christ) and the Holy Spirit, then you are at least acquainted with this mystery. It might be a slightly confusing concept to grasp, but stay with me on this and more will come. No one will understand this grand concept until reaching heaven it is stated, but to know and believe in the Trinity is one of the facets of purpose in life. This is manifested in a person's faith and revealed in the life a person lives. The Catechism of the Catholic Church says this about the Holy Trinity. Section 234, "*The mystery of the Most Holy Trinity is the central mystery of Christian faith and life. It is the mystery of God in himself. It is therefore the source of all the other mysteries of faith, the light that enlightens them. It is the most fundamental and essential teaching in the 'hierarchy of the truths of faith'*".

Embrace the mystery and let it assist you.

The idea of the Holy Trinity sounds confusing to some, but to reassure oneself, the concept of the Holy Trinity is a mystery to all humans. While we do our best with human limitations to know what we can about our often inexplicable, omnipotent and omnificent God, it is still a fact that we cannot understand the fullness of God in this earthly life. We will later do our best to put the Holy Trinity into perspective as well as the concept of our bodies being the temple of the Holy Spirit. It is a mystery that we each have a soul while we live and breathe here on earth, and it resides in our human body, again also the temple of the Holy Spirit. This soul we have carries on a spiritual life into eternity. It can either carry this spiritual life on in great happiness and joy, or it can carry on life in everlasting shame and isolation from God. We want to avoid the latter and strive for the former. "*The Church teaches that every spiritual soul is created immediately by God-it is not "produced" by the parents- and also that it is immortal: it does not perish when it separates from the body at death, and it will be reunited with the body at the final Resurrection*" (Catechism of the Catholic Church, 366).

The awe-inspiring reality regarding the magnitude of the Trinity can never be fully explained or uncovered as deserved in our lifetimes. Contemplating this mystery with the human intellect is simply far from our ability to ever grasp in its entirety. Suffice it to say however, that because of the unfathomable truth that is the Holy Trinity, our limited human thought, desire, and belief regarding our threesome

God pleases Him. Especially when we strive to know all three persons of the Trinity and their separate personhoods. These personhoods being God the Father, God the Son, and God the Holy Spirit. "*We have seen the true Light, we have received the heavenly Spirit, we have found the true faith: we adore the indivisible Trinity, who has saved us*" (Catechism, 732). We will unpack some reasons why the Holy Trinity is important to our purpose in life and to our souls.

Those who have dedicated their entire lives to knowing and serving God (namely celibate religious) may be our best help in realizing the value and purpose of our souls, and hence our lives. One of our purposes and meanings in life is to support our souls so they get to heaven, and this often takes physical, mental, and spiritual endurance. Father Paul O'Sullivan helps us to understand the value of our souls when he states, *"Now let us see the immense value that our souls have in the eyes of God - the care, the love with which God has made them, how He has expended all the riches of His wisdom and power in adorning them and making them worthy residences of the Holy Ghost"* (The Holy Ghost, Our Greatest Friend, pg. 17). Residence of the Holy Spirit? Holy Scripture speaks of our body as a residence, a veritable living space for our God, a temple for the Holy Spirit. God wants to abide in our souls! Whoa…what?!

One can actively be a temple of the Holy Spirit as long as the body and soul are in good standing with God. That is to say, most people do not thrive to harbor evil or commit wickedness in their lives unless one continually prefers the evil. St. John speaks of different kind of sin, and that deadly sin (otherwise known as mortal sin) will separate us from the love of God. This means the Holy Spirit cannot and will not abide in us in a state of mortal sin.

To simply state the principle: *"If you see your brother and sister committing what is not a mortal sin, you will ask and God will give life to such a one-to those whose sin is not mortal. There is sin that is mortal; I do not say that you should pray about that. All wrong-doing is sin, but there is sin that is not mortal"* (1 John 5: 16-17). Having a soul that is eternal (that means it lives in infinity and forever) is a game changer once a person grasps this whole construct. The threshold here however, is that one cannot get to heaven or have the Holy Spirit dwell in your residence if you do not cleanse yourself, or quit doing things that cause this mortal sin. We need to ask ourselves what have we done, and what are we currently doing that is not sanctioned by God. What resolutions do we need to make or how do we convict ourselves to live this life for God.

It is by the strength, perseverance, and endurance that the reader is to overcome this sin. If one is already a Catholic and has received the Sacrament of Penance, then that soul should exercise the sacrament to remove all mortal sin, the sin that can separate oneself from God for all eternity. This is a big deal to acknowledge and know that one has committed mortal sin in their life, and refuse to do anything to be forgiven. Many excuse themselves from being in this type of sin because they do not want to change their lifestyle or admit what they did was wrong. Pride of this type is blinding. Make no mistake, we are either winners or losers in this life. The winners take those precautions and actions that make them follow the will of God, and be forgiven of sin. The losers either ignore or refuse to acknowledge and take action towards following the will of God and do not believe they need to ask God for forgiveness and change their ways.

The way we treat our temples can lead us to realizing our greatest reward is heaven provided we do good and repent from evil. To repent means to make amend and acknowledge our wrong actions and thoughts, while having a state of mind that does not want to further commit evil. In other words, we need to have a desire not to sin. If we keep sinning and choosing the ways of the world, this could prove to be our temple and soul's final demise to hell. Especially if one elects to continue to sin and the warning to stop this behavior goes unheeded. The fact that we are a temple, a dwelling place for our

God, alone makes us worthy in His eyes as he desires to be close to us. Remember, we are trying to reciprocate this dwelling place both physically and spiritually by making our final destination heaven as our dwelling place. *"Or do you not know that your body is a temple of the Holy Spirit within you, which you have from God, and that you are not your own? For you were bought with a price; therefore, glorify God in your body"* (1 Corinthians 6: 19-20).

The fact that God wishes to be close to us and desires to dwell within us is an amazing notion in and of itself. It gives us a glimpse of God's love for us. It is a direct reflection of how much we are treasured by our God and thus that much more of a prized and unique possession for Him. We will expand on the premise that we are cherished and how fortunate we are to be the temple of the Holy Spirit. We will conclude in the recognition that this alone is enough reason for purpose in life in and of itself. We keep the idea of achieving that heavenly dwelling place each day.

The effort put forth to know our Lord Jesus pays dividends now and forever.

Contemplating the life of our Lord and Savior Jesus Christ and all He completed while with us, leads us to also study His character traits in strength, perseverance, and endurance. For those of you who do not yet know Him, you can and will. If you authentically pray the following simple prayer to Him for ten days, ten times a day with a focused and non-distracted mindset, and with the true intent of learning how much He cares about you, He will reveal Himself by you opening your heart to this desire. *"Jesus Christ, my Lord and Savior, by your holy and precious blood, reveal your love for me!"* You will begin to experience and feel an inner draw to get closer to Him and will desire to know more about Him. It's a life changer!

It is that desire to know Him, this longing for God is something we will continue to desire until we are with Him in the afterlife. This writing, however, will give a dimension to Jesus's Holy attributes that you will not only be able to relate to, but the hope is that you will emulate and understand that He can help provide these same attributes to you to assist you through daily life. Besides receiving Jesus daily in the Eucharist, (A Catholic Sacrament that is the essence of our existence) we try and become more "Christ-like" in our own actions and personality. Jesus is often looked upon for His wisdom, love, forgiveness, and rightly so, however, our "all providing God" in His dual nature also demonstrated some virtues that we can also emulate and take from that to get us through each day.

It is the authors' attempt at trying to highlight some of these virtues, ones that are a potentially overlooked or not considered regarding our Lord. Virtues that can very much help others to reflect upon and pattern their own challenges, sufferings, and ordeals. It is in modeling these virtues that many are provided the encouragement and will to follow in His example.

However, one can also more confidently pray to Him to give you a more substantial amount of these graces called virtues. One can ask for more of a portion of these three virtues when people are contending with life's overpowering circumstances. Finally, we will explore some of the heroic lives of others and the sufferings, hardships, and afflictions they undertook while exhibiting these main three virtues. It is the hope that the reader can then apply some of their own grit in taking on life.

"Count it all joy, my brothers, when you fall into various temptations, knowing that the testing of your faith produces endurance. Let endurance have its perfect work, that you may be perfect and complete, lacking in nothing."

(Letter to St. James 1:2-4)

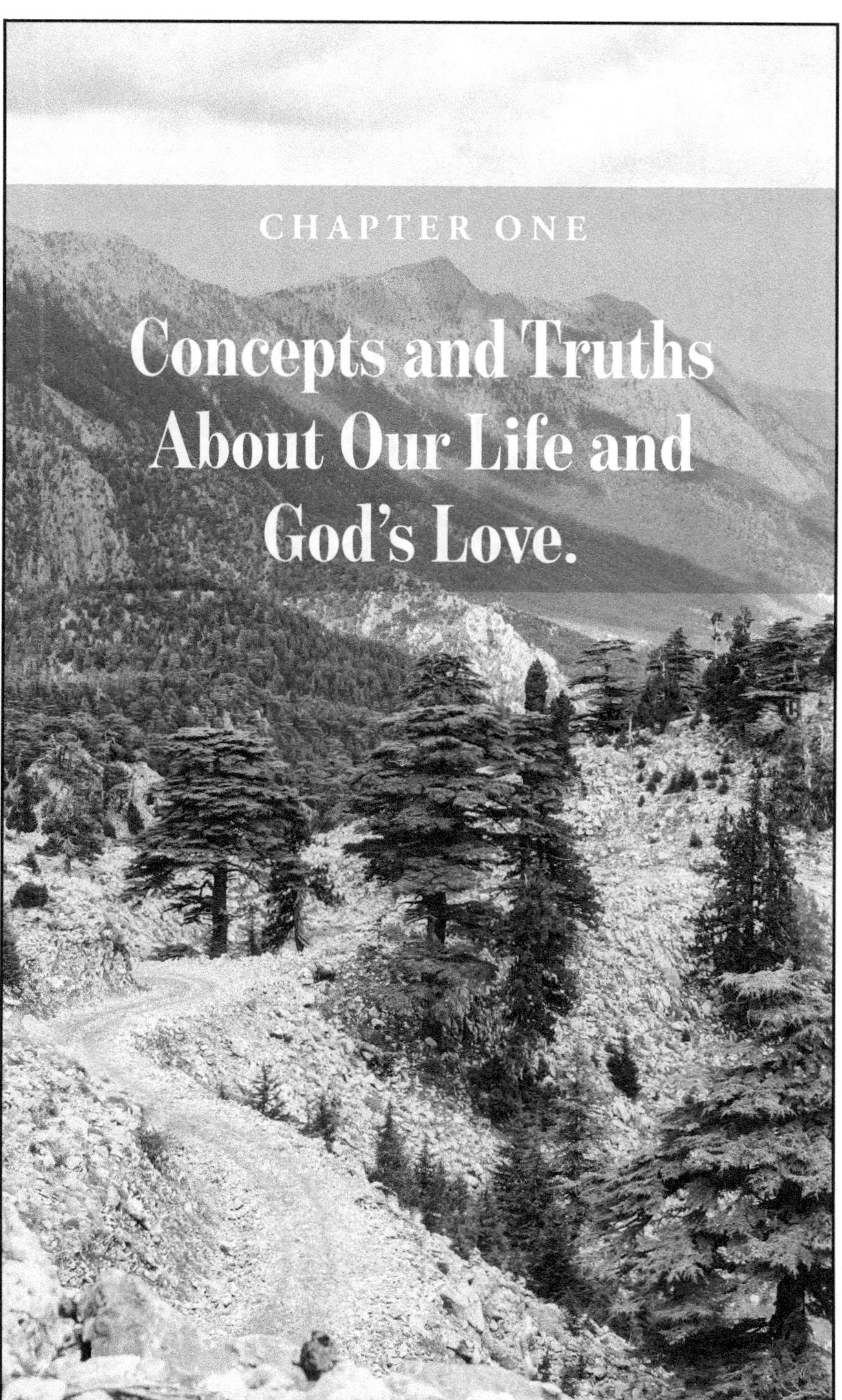

CHAPTER ONE

Concepts and Truths About Our Life and God's Love.

Our Lord is simply amazing and wants to help us.

I would ask you to consider some of the reasons and purpose for reading this simple book. It is my humble observation and belief that Our Lord has some amazing attributes that were exemplified in virtues that are often overlooked. The examples He provided while on earth are to be recollected, drawn upon to emulate, and reproduced and interjected into our own life's circumstances. These qualities and features of our Lord's own virtues are recalled to help us get through this life. Bringing these virtues to the forefront where people are contemplating and meditating on what Jesus demonstrated for us is the goal. Reflecting upon and aspiring to imitate these manifested virtues in our own lives, (namely His Holy strength, perseverance, and endurance) we can then be inspired to live these virtues as well. First, we must request through prayer that He might bestow these virtues upon us through his grace and providence. We are to mimic these to show our dedication to passing life's test and following Jesus's example to get to the dwelling place in heaven. This should be your ultimate life's purpose, if it is not already.

The main reason for the accumulation of examples and references in this narrative is to point to our Lord's example, and obtain some confidence in asking Him for help with our daily difficulties. Our nature is such that we may be apt to give up from shear exhaustion and in "throwing in the towel" so to speak, from being overwhelmed with worldly demands and daunting pressures. It is easy to understand how beat down, how empty, and how much life can dole out to those who are single, married, and with religious vocations alike. The author grasps the notion of how one can struggle to find any meaning at all, and go through life resorting to other often unhealthy means to continue with daily survival. Drugs and pain killers, gambling, promiscuous sexual behavior, and or the unhealthy pursuit of power and money only lead to more confusion and true slavery of oneself to the evil one.

We were never meant to deal with life on our own.

Unfortunately, stress and sorrow can bring one to despair such that resorting to the above vices mentioned or worse yet, ending one's own life, might be seen as the easiest way to provide relief from the crushing hurt. The author in no way advocates ending one's life, but rather understands that this is a real temptation for some, however it is never the solution! Jesus is way bigger than any problem you or I have and He will help you remedy any issues.

Sometimes the unending pain that one experiences all day, every day, brings one to question the reason for existing or why we are here? Understanding the cycle of misery and hopelessness firsthand, some insight and assistance can be made here. Some of us have lived harsh existences. It is the desire to help deliver and liberate others from this devastating weight and pain and help people know there is relief and purpose. This writing's content is presented to help you reach out to Jesus Christ who will be your reprieve from the storm. It is beyond time you get to know Him if you do not already know Him. He willingly went to the cross and shed his blood specifically for you. He would do this all over again if it was you or I alone that needed saving. This is how much we are loved!

The result of His death, sacrifice, and resurrection from the dead puts His name above any other name by God the Father. Jesus is truly the King of the Universe and beyond! This power He received from

God the Father after doing the Father's will is demonstrated time and again in defying death, in the presentation of countless miracles, and His mighty victory against all evil.

The Mighty and Holy name of Jesus

We need to learn to speak the language of heaven and claim the victory in His powerful Name. The Catholic Church so much honors the holy and powerful name of Jesus, that it celebrates the *Name of Jesus* every January 3rd. We need to reverently and unapologetically call out on the name of Jesus on our own behalf. It is the name of Jesus that every knee will eventually bend to and worship. This name of Jesus is to be used to claim victory over many things in our life that hinder our holiness and make us worry. He is above all others and will come to your rescue time and again!

In the Gospel of St. John, we are told this regarding what St. John the Baptist (not to be confused with St. John the apostle), testified to us so we could have some authenticity as to whom Jesus was and is. He tells us of Jesus, *"I saw the Spirit descending from heaven like a dove, and it remained on him. I myself did not know him, but the one who sent me to baptize with water said to me, 'He on whom you see the Spirit descend and remain is the one who baptizes with the Holy Spirit.' And I myself have seen and testified that this is the Son of God".* (John 1: 32-34). We have a firsthand eye witness in St. John's testimony regarding who Jesus is. As a natural result, we can take to heart what St. Paul tells us in his letter to the Phillipians 2:10, about the power of Jesus's name. *"Therefore, God also highly exalted him and gave him the name that is above every name , so that at the name of Jesus every knee should bend, in heaven and on earth and under the earth, and every tongue should confess that Jesus Christ is Lord to the glory of God the Father"*. We need to ask our Lord to help prompt us to remember to use His name for help!

We need to ultimately learn to do the will of God in our own lives to the point where it becomes our only focus. In the name of our Lord and Savior Jesus Christ one can claim the power of our Lord. *"Whatever you ask in my name, this I will do, that the Father may be glorified in the Son. If you ask me anything in my name, I will do it"* (John 14: 13-14). He protects you from the deadly downpour of the hailstones of grief, sadness, and despair that can otherwise eventually pound you to submission. *" We are to live in His Victory and be people that live this victory rather than live lives of depression, anxiety, anger and hurt"* (Mrs. Vicky Smith, Mystic and Healer, 2025).

Vicky Smith's ministry is called the Upper Room Ministry. She is someone you will want to talk to if you have ongoing hurt, physical ailments , or depression. She will help you understand the power of our Lord Jesus Christ. (Inonespirit.com). I promise you will not be sorry you researched this website. Vicky communicates on a very intimate level with our Lord and is a powerful intercessor. It is her ministry to intercede and pray for people, and is what she does in her dedication to our Lord. She and her prayer team make for powerful intercessors and she will help educate you in speaking the language of heaven. One of her favorite verses' is from Proverbs 18 vs. 21 *"Death and life are in the power of the tongue, and those who love it will eat its fruits".* Learn this language and help transform your lives! It is also super important to remember not to use our Lord's name in vain and honor the third commandment. Remember, it is a serious sin to swear our Lord's name, even in a casual manner. This is how serious it is regarding the name of Jesus. So, let us honor His name and claim victory over whatever it is that is ailing us. The evil spirits of affliction cannot withstand the Holy and Mighty name of Jesus!

Understanding the need to emulate Jesus and rely on Him more

One of the main facets of this writing is to promote the holy virtues of Jesus's strength, perseverance and endurance in order that others continue the good fight against evil forces in their lives. It is time to recover (and then some), what the devil has literally stolen from us. Society has had a very dark last century until now. The last five to ten years have taken their toll. Covid 19 sent the world into a despair, and it demonstrated that governments do not always have the best interests in mind for their peoples, and the coldness of people's heart is a tangible reality. It is a sobering but real fact. We as a society need to overcome this darkness by calling out to Jesus, and asking His Blessed Mother (The Immaculate Virgin Mary whom we will learn more about as the writing continues) to help us dedicate ourselves to Him.

With that theme in mind, it is our time in the history of the world for us (you and I created here and now) to focus our gaze on Jesus Christ before anything else. People need to realize that through our own sin and selfishness, we open doors that allow the evil one to take and steal from us and drag us down. It is time to stop that plundering in our lives. Understand that the Blessed Mother Mary most Holy is one who intercedes for us (who brings our issues to Jesus and asks Him too to help us). We will study more on how we can request the Holy Virgin, Jesus's Mother, to help us get to Jesus even closer than we could on our own. Trust for now that this is true and in time you will understand more!

Chapter One

Harnessing Two Thousand years of teachings, principles and beliefs

One thing is critical that the reader consider when encapsulating all we are discussing about our Lord and all His plans. This is that many of the teachings presented here in this writing come from catechism (or instructions) that helps sort out truth from non-truth. Catechism is basically two thousand years of tradition, scripture, and liturgy that give us many definitions, principles, beliefs, and facts. This book uses the Catholic Catechism as based on the Holy Church that Jesus founded. He entrusted the handing down of his Church and teachings to hand chosen men that were like you and I. These men kept "succession" happening and soon many people entered the Church and it continued to grow to the largest faith in the world. These men developed the catechism with the help of God's Holy Spirit.

This same Catechism is one of the sources used in our reading that I ask the reader to trust in, and at the same time to definitely reference and understand the meanings quoted. The term *Catechism* is defined as, *"Something that helps us understand the meaning of what Jesus Christ has taught and it requires that we are trying to learn about Christ Himself at the same time."* Catechism is age old and it helps us understand what has been handed down through history regarding truths of our Lord through sacred scripture and liturgy. This catechism helps us learn things about good and evil and the age-old battle. It can help us sort out our own lives when we are lost, hurt, disappointed, mad, and dejected. It helps us understand our purpose.

Realize that you are in the fight for your eternal soul!

Sometimes we do not even realize why we are angry, frustrated or cannot get above certain constraints. Sometimes we cannot get past our own self-issues. It is often spiritual and emotional healing we need and we need to use all of heaven's gifts that are being offered to us to fight and take back that which was stolen from us by the evil one. Do you have a void in your life that you cannot put your finger on? It is because the devil tries to take us further and further from our Lord. It is time to have this trend reversed in your life and time to gain back this ground in a war you do not even realize you are fighting. Let us go to the scriptures, to the Catechism, to what other saints have learned, and to what other sources say regarding how to fill this void. It all comes back to learning about Jesus and His love for us. He loves you and you might not grasp this yet?

Consider this. The evil one succeeds when he murders our goodness, when he murders our intent to love one another, when he murders our ability to love God above all things. When the evil one (the devil) tempts us with worldly goods and pleasures, we betray ourselves and trade in our spiritual goodness for worldly junk. Jesus says this of him, *"He was a murderer from the beginning and does not stand in the truth, because there is no truth in him"* (John 8 , 44). In the foreword, we asked the reader to trust in learning certain spiritual truths. This is one of those truths. The devil is real, and he is fighting God with his demons to take your soul! Do not let him win! Fight back with all your moral strength! Because he murders our love for God and neighbor, we not only ask Jesus to give us the grace to overcome this evil, but we show our sincerity and love for God by trying to make up for our failings and faults.

Small offerings back to God start us down the path of sainthood

One of these means to correct our failures and sinfulness is by offering sacrifice and mortifications. The smallest things offered back to the Lord in atonement for our sins is very pleasing to our Lord. It gains us back some spiritual ground that we have forfeited with sinfulness. We will learn more about saints and their lives as the book goes on, but suffice it to say that saints are highly favored people because their whole lives were to serve and do everything for our Lord. They sacrificed and atoned not only for themselves but for other people to gain grace and overcome their sinful ways.

The saints give us a great example of how to love Jesus. Therefore, some of the examples used going forward involve the lives of the saints as there are no better examples we have, and no better friends of ours in heaven to help us get to Jesus. The definition of a saint is someone who has gone before us in the faith that the Catholic Church recognizes is in heaven, and therefore is worthy to ask assistance from, worthy to have them intercede for you and your needs on earth. So, with that in mind, Jesus often spoke to these saints interiorly and they received special grace to do what Jesus was asking of them. They can and will assist us if we ask them to do so, much like the above reference to the Blessed Virgin Mary who is the Queen of Heaven and Heaven's chief saint. We will learn more as the book continues.

Let's consider Saint Sister Faustina Kowalska. The first saint of the 21st century, a highly favored person. Jesus said to St. Faustina, while a nun in Poland, a religious of the order of the Congregation of the Sisters of Our Lady of Mercy, *"Daughter, I need sacrifice lovingly accomplished because that alone has meaning for Me. Enormous indeed are the debts of the world which are due to Me.; pure souls can pay them by their sacrifice, exercising mercy in spirit"* (Mercy My Mission, pg. 176). For the last fifty plus years, maybe sixty, our concept of sacrifice as a society has been reduced to this spiritual necessity almost becoming non-existent in the culture. People need to atone for their sins. If they cannot do that, it will prove a miserable existence.

Sacrifice and suffering are components to obtaining virtue

Very few people realize or want to realize the power of sacrifice and "offering" our suffering back to the Lord both for reparation (repairing for our injustice towards God and His charity) of our sins, but for making amends to God for others as well. Yes, we have to make amends or repair for the damage done by our sins. We can either do this in this life or in another state called purgatory after we die (this is a concept for another time, but a topic the reader needs to trust in for now). In other words, offering deeds of mercy and selflessness in the forms of kindness, goodness, and sacrifice back to God help atone for our shortcomings and selfish failures. If through people's suffering and trials they can learn the concept of atonement, (one that the devil has worked so hard for people to forget because it keeps us drawn away from Jesus), they can start to get the upper hand on the evil one! Remember this well. We need to gain back the lost ground in our spiritual lives. Suffering will crystalize your love for the Holy Trinity.

The reality is that there is abundant value in "offering up" the distress, misery, agony, and grieving that one is undergoing or has undergone back to the Lord. There is actually a name for it. This offering sacrifice and penance (we will learn more about these concepts later) back to the Lord is referred to as *redemptive suffering*. If you can harness these sacrificial practices and be in the mind-frame to verbally and mentally "give these tangible and intangible donations back to God" as a charity to Him, you are obtaining a spiritual grace that literally has endless value. I mean infinite value when you understand this concept, because these actions follow you into eternity. Yes, suffering has much merit for this life and the next. He can use this suffering not only to make your life more purified and to obtain graces that strengthen and fortify you, but you can actually prevent souls (most especially your own soul) from going to hell. This is a mystery from Jesus, and is why He is such an awesome God for us! You can obtain the mercy needed to lessen your own Judgement. (Mercy My Mission, pg. 176). These are hard concepts to understand right now, but as time goes on, and grace continues to accumulate in your soul, these spiritual gifts become more sought after. We are going to look at our Lord's example of the three virtues that he demonstrates that can help us continue to get the upper hand on evil.

Remember, we need to fight the devil constantly, because, whether you were told this or not in the past, the devil's main motive is to steal your soul from God whom he hates. This is why there is an epic battle that one cannot see that is spiritually taking place all the time and does not cease! This is why you need to be aware that your soul is what is being fought for and the souls of all mankind are in the balance. This is a serious and imminent truth and therefore if you do not learn anything else from this book, learn to cry out to Jesus and consecrate your life to Him now and ask him for the help to understand how to Love Him moving forward. He will help you!

He has already conquered death and the war with the devil, but as in any war, the battle still rages for the "goods" and "property". Your soul is that property, and it belongs to God.

Discover how much your Heavenly Mother loves you

As promised, we need to discuss the Blessed Virgin Mary's role in all this. The Mother of Christ and our adoptive Mother, begs this from each of us in requesting these sufferings, prayers, and fasting as sacrifice.

"No sacrifice is too small for the Lord to use as good" (Vicky Smith, author, mystic and healer in the name of Jesus, O Crux Ave Media, 2024). Imagine if you are partially responsible for being eternally helpful to someone you have assisted (with God's omnipotent mercy) to get to heaven. Mary is responsible for giving us our Salvation. She gave us Jesus. She has had an awesome role in helping us get to heaven and She is not done helping us if we ask Her. When you think of it, our Blessed Mother is the Heroine of the world besides Jesus. Protestants are coming around in their rethinking on the Blessed Mother's role in salvation history. Many Protestants, not all of course, believe that by honoring the Blessed Mother as Catholics do, that this somehow threatens the Kingship of Jesus? In reality it is 180 degrees the contrary. Remember, Catholics honor the Blessed Mother, and rightly so, but they do not worship Her. There is an infinity of difference in the two definitions. Only God is worthy of our worship. Our Blessed Mother Mary, however, points us to Jesus the whole time and comes to our assistance to get to know Her son. She understands our eternity is decided upon whether or not we ultimately accept Jesus or not.

She wants us to obtain this personal relationship with Jesus. Where Jesus is, she is spiritually present too. Another mystery to fathom! Please remember the following important fact. If it were not for our Blessed Mother saying "Yes" to God's request for Her to become the Mother of the savior, (sometimes referred to as her fiat through the angel Gabriel and ultimately to God the Father to bring Jesus into the world), there would be no Jesus Christ our redeemer and savior. She calls us to have a relationship with Herself as well, as she wants to teach us more about Her son. If you invite Her into your life, it will be one of the best decisions you ever make.

While concepts regarding the saints interceding for us is something many Protestant churches struggle with, (as discussed above), we still must compensate for our sinfulness. This requires mentioning again. This is truth, and is revealed by Jesus who is Truth itself. More on this later, but this is partially the reason St. James teaches us that works and faith are necessary for salvation. "*What good is it, my brothers and sisters, if you say you have faith but do not have works? Can faith save you?*" (James 2:14).

This is where Jesus's examples are introduced. Our Lord showed us how to live a life full of good works and taught us to have faith in Him and God the Father. He demonstrated how to overcome many adversities with his strength, perseverance, and endurance. This is what we will soon focus on, but these above concepts are necessary for understanding your purpose on earth to get to the heavenly realm. He wants us to produce "good fruit" and we do so with completing good works on earth. With doing good, we avoid and reject all intrinsically evil things and learn about these evils as we progress in our mental spirituality. No evil means can ever justify an end result.

Remember that you grow in your spirituality and do so by continuing to do good always.

God's providence in relation to our purpose

It is significant that people understand that whatever kind of life path they have chosen, they have a purpose. While it might not seem important, God has a plan for their lives. It is referred to as the providence of God. While many other books could be written on that topic alone, it is noteworthy to believe in His promises and protections in the providence He has in our lives.

Yes, God works in our lives. He wants to be active in what we do. It is not so much what people accomplish in earthly measures (however what we do is still important), but rather how they remain faithful to God throughout the long term. We have to invite Jesus in to every decision we make until it becomes habit to do so. It is the desire to want to do the right thing and serve Him in all we undertake. This is difficult to grasp when nothing seems to go right, when we are struggling with life, and when things do not go as planned. Sometimes a defeating thought crosses the mind. *"What purpose does life have at all for me"?* When this happens, one needs to step back and understand that you are being tempted by the devil to despair. Do not let him do this to you, but rather call out to Jesus to help you do what He wants you to do at that time.

This is why knowing and believing in God's oversight, and experiencing His love and kindness, are ways that bring about purpose to everyone's life. This is where our awesome God quarterbacks our lives if we let Him. We need to give things over to Him and ask Him for help. Practice saying "Jesus I Trust in You". We will come back to this concept.

"But about that day and hour no one knows, neither the angels of heaven, nor the Son, but only the Father. For as the days of Noah were, so will be the coming of the Son of Man." (Matthew, 24, 36-37). Various mystics, (those who have special insights and knowledge from God) have stated that we live in a time more sinful than the Great Flood that wiped out all but eight people from the face of the earth. Mystics are those who are privileged to obtain certain prophecies from God, just as there were prophets in the Old and New Testament times. There are still people who God chooses to speak through. This is another truth the reader needs to be open to.

Many people do not believe in the story of Noah, but ironically many in Noah's time also thought nothing would ever become of their immoral and wicked lifestyles. The day came for those in Noah's time and it was a bad ending. It is very meaningful to try and fulfill God's will, as tomorrow may or may not come. If you are striving each day to be holy, to increase in faith and to give back to God what is His (namely love to Him and to our fellow human), to repent and convert from any sinfulness, and to not give up with all one faces, then you are doing what is asked of you. If you are doing these things with love then you are doing God's will. These are the first steps on your path to the heavenly dwelling place.

One of the best Gospel promises from Jesus

What is important to remember is that you are not alone in your day-to-day sufferings and what you have to endure. It is then critical to keep asking our Lord for His help and it will come. Jesus gives us Himself as an example of doing God's will even when it costs Him everything. He also promises us He will never leave us orphaned. That means you can call on Him to get you through these sufferings and to legitimately expect help. If people are resisting an errant and corrupt way of life, but rather are striving to keep coming back to God for his assistance, that divine help will arrive. "*Ask and will be given to you, search, and you will find; knock, and the door will be opened for you*" (Matthew 7,7). People need encouragement and examples. People need to be reminded that God will improve their situation for sure! Let us start to consider what it means to ask our Lord for His assistance.

God is love. Probably the most underrated concept of all time. People have lost all concept of our God and that He loves us to the point of having created us for Himself. Have you ever asked yourself why God created you? It is because He loves us and wants to adopt us. He actually wants us to share in the life His true Son has purchased for us with His death and resurrection. We really would not have much to live for if we did not believe that God sent His son to recover the ability to enter into the kingdom of heaven. Why believe in Jesus at all if we did not believe He conquered death and lives as our King now? Jesus shows us a way of life that pleases God.

There really is not much point at all to Christianity without these concepts and truths. This is the reason we are studying our own purpose and how we fit into God's plan in the eternal Kingdom. This is why we need to start considering and acknowledging that God loves us. He wills it for us to be blessed, joyful, and productive children of His. For these reasons, He deserves our praise and worship each day. He deserves us trying to be good and for us to do His will.

Doing good everyday

Our lives are to "bear good fruit". God hopes for us and expects us to be people that are doing good things with our lives despite struggles and challenges. He gives us those virtues of strength, perseverance, and endurance to continue onward each day. God is patient with us, but again he expects from us good works towards one another. He expects us to show love and generosity and reflect our Heavenly Father's genuine and authentic goodness.

Consider the story of the fig tree in the bible. Jesus comes across a fig tree and He looks it up and down for some figs. He is looking for the tree to give Him some fruit, something good. Fig trees are usually mature by their third year and start to produce figs. If they do not produce in this timeframe, they risk getting cut down because they will probably not ever produce. God gives us time to do good things in this life. Some of us get longer time than others. The point is that we need to eventually, sooner than later, come forward and have some good fruit to offer God. Otherwise, we are just taking up space in this world.

Good things offered back to God can come in a wide variety of things that please Him. From prayers, to offering charitable acts, to doing anonymous works that support others are all examples of pleasing gifts to Him. Engaging in these acts for others takes our minds off ourselves and gives us purpose. This purpose starts to eventually create a desire for our own reserved spot in the heavenly dwelling place. Are these presented concepts and truths starting to "connect the dots"?

Then He told this parable: " *'A man had a fig tree planted in his vineyard; and he came looking for fruit on it and found none. So he said to the gardener, 'See here!' For three years I have come looking for fruit on this fig tree, and still I find none. Cut it down! Why should it be wasting the soil?' He replied, 'Sir, let it alone for one more year, until I dig round it and put manure on it. If it bears fruit next year, well and good; but if not, you can cut it down.'"* (Luke 13 vs. 6-9). We have no reason to be "wasting the soil" in our lives. We have many opportunities to produce some good things for God. Let us get going on these opportunities and reflect on our God's love for us!

Humbling ourselves and asking for help

The author of this writing has also had some very serious spiritual and physical struggles in life. As a matter of fact, as this is being written, there are many challenges I face each day. I live in full the reality of daily suffering, but it motivates me to continue on. After having to learn to rely on God's omnipotent intervention, it is powerfully motivating to want to help others comprehend how much our God loves us. I find myself welled up with tears of thankfulness and joy that God has pulled me through some extremely difficult scenarios. He has carried me through some dark valleys that I thought resembled hell on earth. Through all this I am here to tell you that I have surrendered everything and now just live for Him and all that He is asking me to contribute to His Kingdom that is already here. Remember that we just need to "CLAIM THE VICTORY" that Jesus has already won. If you listen, you will be asked to live with your soul in heaven while you complete your duties and responsibilities of the flesh here on earth until the time comes for your reward.

Some of us are still very much trying to learn about His extraordinary love and mercy more each day. God's love is demonstrated in His incredible mercy. Sometimes prayer can include begging our Lord to assist us with whatever it is that we need deliverance from. Fr. Chad Ripperger, a Catholic priest and exorcist, has compiled a book called *Deliverance Prayers* and it is a must reading. These prayers request God's assistance in suppressing evil and are significantly powerful. Fr. Ripperger is very "matter of fact", but stresses the power of prayer.

Reciting these prayers help us get a foothold again back towards choosing the Holy Trinity. For whatever reason, sometimes the devil gets a stranglehold on us. The evil one gets a sort of choke hold on us. We then need Jesus's power and blessings mainly through his priests and mystics. These are to whom He has given authority and spiritual gifts to respectively. He helps us out of these spiritual chains and afflictions by literally making the demons flee.

It is critical to call out to our Lord Jesus for help whenever you start to feel helpless. Calling on the name of Jesus, or requesting Jesus's precious blood to cover the situation is powerful and will send the demons screaming and crying away from us. The sign of the cross is something everyone should learn. It should always be used reverently and can be used often to bless oneself in times of temptation, especially when one needs to be delivered from that moment. The sign of the cross has much power and signing oneself can bring blessings to one's soul. Suffice it to remember that the devil wants to take your soul away from God because God loves it. He hates God, and does not want God to win the fight for your soul. Remember that!

Jesus's help in overcoming these strains and fights put a desire in our hearts to show why Jesus is truly our Lord and Divine hero. We ultimately surrender to Him, Jesus (See Surrender Novena in the appendices, by Fr. Dolindo Ruotolo), and become strong in our weakness. Jesus becomes our strength. He is love and love conquers all.

There is a reason why people call on Catholic Priests in time of spiritual turmoil

Has it ever occurred to you that in cases where someone needs deliverance from oppression and/or possession, they do not rely on Protestant pastors or shamans to come to the rescue? Rather they call a Catholic priest who is trained in exorcism, because that priest is from the lineage of the Apostles (the Bishops that Jesus instituted himself). Bishops are actually exorcists by the power of Christ Jesus, and they often designate priests under their authority to be exorcists for the Diocese (their area of jurisdiction in the Church). Oh yeah, they call in the big guns. These priests are the real deal as far as who Christ Jesus appointed His authority to on earth. They take care of business and put the devil to flight. The afflicted person is able to spiritually recover. Sometimes this takes more than one exorcism for the afflicted person.

The facts do not lie, but one needs to be open to the truth

It should demonstrate to everyone and be evidence of where the true Church is from. Yes, the Catholic Church is the Church that Jesus founded. There is evidence all over history regarding this fact. He loved us so much he died for us, but in so doing created the Catholic Church. From this founding came the men He chose to succeed Him on earth and give us His sacraments. The devil knows where this true authority comes from and he hates the Catholic Church. Again, it is God's love for us that He demonstrates the might of His Holy Arm through His appointed priests. He comes to our rescue through others He has appointed, or directly by His Own Holy volition.

Finally, it is important to provide some practical and real-life thoughts and examples of how ordinary people (including those of some saints) have furnished us with gripping examples of how they have overcome trials and tribulations. Again, many times we bring upon ourselves struggles, but other times the evil one is permitted to test us.

God asks us to prove that we love Him. He also wants to test our faith in Him. This makes us worthy. It is part of our purpose in life. Faith and love ultimately help us demonstrate the above-mentioned virtues. God allows evil, but has power over the evil. Therefore, we ask Him to fight our battles for us. *"For our struggle is not against enemies of blood and flesh but against the rulers, against authorities, against the cosmic powers of this present darkness, against the spiritual forces of evil in the heavenly places".* (Ephesians 6, 12). Yes, we fight a spiritual fight and we need to fight with spiritual weapons such as calling on the name of Jesus and making use of the sacraments of the Catholic Church. For those who are not yet members of the Church this writing will continue to give examples of how to fight spiritually. Spiritual warfare is a critical concept and truth that needs to be learned. Learning how to defeat evil will give you great confidence towards your purpose in life.

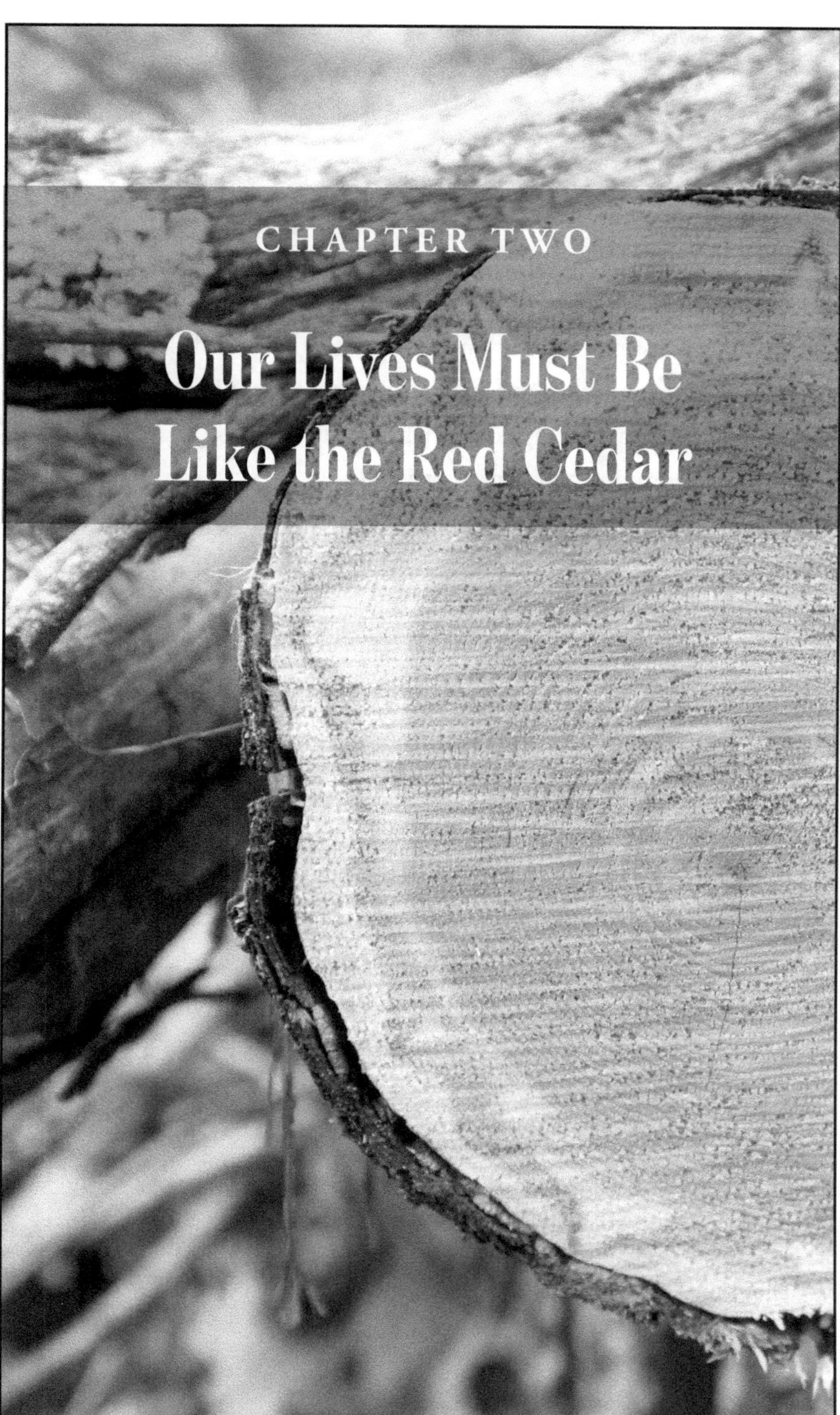

CHAPTER TWO

Our Lives Must Be Like the Red Cedar

Often people can relate to things by providing for them a visual image of something as an analogy. Sometimes describing things in detail can help them relate to someone's point. Often the way people envision something in their minds is the way it is described in full. This is the point of the next example.

It important to have people contemplate all the attributes they might acquire that may make their lives and their personal traits enhanced and more able to do good. Sometimes people are inspired when they can see themselves as something of great value, or that their lives are beautiful, and that someone else finds worth in their overall personhood. This is healthy because all life is extremely beautiful from what God has created.

The point is that God does not create any life that does not reflect His excellence in some manner. Human life can become tainted because of the weight of sin and this is manifested in many aspects. However, one can strive to be noble and demonstrate virtuous character and personality traits that motivate others to display similar virtuous features. In this brief illustration, try and understand that people's displayed actions and demeanor demonstrate whether they are producing good fruit and love towards God. If people are not interested in this, it shows up fairly fast and is exposed in a short time knowing that individual. This is why we strive to be those people, those Christians that authentically act and behave like Jesus.

We are required to help one another

We need to help bolster one another and help everyone see their own great value as an adopted child of our heavenly Father. Everyone needs to eventually come to the realization that God loves them. Sometimes we need a real-life example of what we want our lives to look like and emulate that example.

We need to follow the example of Jesus because He demonstrates to us the virtues needed to combat a world that tempts us to do the exact opposite. Jesus demonstrated the virtues of strength, perseverance, and endurance in many facets. He showed us how to live these virtues out in times that were challenging and remarkably unfavorable. He committed doing good the whole while He was on earth. We need to become more like Him, we need to become like an evergreen tree which is fragrant, one that contributes to the forest of God.

The aromatic Red Cedar (Juniperus virginiana) is a slow growing coniferous evergreen tree that grows throughout the midwestern United States. It can grow to 60- 70 feet when mature, and thrives particularly well in some counties of Minnesota where there is well draining sandy ground. The red cedar has a tap root that makes the tree very susceptible to dying once it becomes severed. It does not take well to replanting once established. It houses many nests and varieties of birds in its younger years, and as it grows, it grows straight and strong. It is a hardwood that is very disease resistant and makes for amazingly beautiful wood used in many natural and rustic looking décor. Its branches are often made into tools such as handles and walking sticks for hiking. The birds use this tree to make its nests because it is so sturdy and apt to defend against adverse weather. Its foliage is thick and woven and provides for good shelter.

The wood of the red cedar is very strong and can be used for beams and posts. It has an aroma that is unlike any other tree, making it very valuable for certain furniture drawers, clothes chests, and closets. While the tree is ancient and its descendants follow the river paths and lakes areas, some do not see its value and claim it to be an invasive species. Some are ignorant of its true history and its relation to the massive cedars on the west coast including the Sequoias. The red cedar grows straight and has tender shoots that grow out each spring. These tender shoots give the tree a bluish appearance and soft texture. While it is a slow growing species, very few diseases effect its growing and therefore it is a very unique tree.

This tree endures the harsh winters in the upper Midwest of North America where temps can get a low as minus 40 degrees windchill in winters and 100 degrees or more Fahrenheit in the summer months. It is adaptable to these climate swings and also is strong against straight line winds and snowfalls. With all of these remarkable qualities of plant species perseverance, endurance, and strength, this tree commands for itself a place in nature that all should recognize. It has incredible adaptability, resilience and outright fortitude in a natural sense. The life of the red cedar demonstrates durability to the elements and all that challenges its existence. At the same time produces great resources through its wood and stability as a tree for society. It provides a protective and comfortably secure home to animals. The red cedar has all the qualities we need to possess to help others and to do the will of God for ourselves.

Qualities that become Christ-like

This tree is analogous to the life of our Lord Jesus Christ here on earth. He was both divine and human and demonstrated to us the qualities to overcome all types of conditions and tests, harsh treatments, and extreme requirements. He, much like the red cedar is the example for our lives. We need to strive to exhibit and display the virtues and characteristics of the red cedar. We look at Jesus's example and pray that we might imitate and become that red cedar to others in pursuing our purpose in life.

This purpose is to serve God by doing His most Holy and perfect will even though real-world circumstances and situations are inhospitable and bleak. The cedar acts as a shelter and home for others. It is when we are in these harsh and barren conditions that we need Jesus to help us fulfill our purpose. Sometimes we are called upon to be that shelter for others, that protecting person that comes to someone's rescue because we are strong and can persevere and endure for them.

By serving God, we gain these good qualities like the red cedar. Serving others provides for us purpose to do good and points us back to God who is all good. It points us to wanting to do even more benevolent acts. It points us to wanting to be with God. This helps us achieve growing closer to Him and eventually making our way to our ultimate dwelling place with Him in heaven. Do you feel like your daily actions provide good for yourself and others? Are you interested in cultivating these virtues to become more of a spiritual red cedar?

As we explore the purpose for our lives, we look closer at our Lord's perfect example. We set our sights on becoming a red cedar with its regal stature and attractive aroma. That tree that provides for others not only a model in character, but shelter and relief for those in our lives we experience that also need to know purpose. Much like the red cedar, we need to demonstrate the virtues of endurance, perseverance, and strength that assist us in fulfilling the Will of God in our lives.

Jesus is Love Itself!

We look to emulate Jesus Christ our risen Lord who exhibited and established a standard in these three virtues. By doing so, it helps us discover and understand the meaning of Love. Jesus is Love itself!

What He did for us and how He accomplished it speaks to the immeasurably infinite amount He cares for and wants to be with us. To be worthy of this Divine Love one must exhibit the same virtues, and therefore truly learn the purpose of our lives. Let us get started to understand and learn of our Lord's cedar-like qualities you may have not considered!

CHAPTER THREE

To Know Him, Love Him, and Serve Him

When nothing that you do in your daily lives seems to matter or be of any value or worth, it is time to start focusing on assisting others. If we are continually "down in the dumps" why would we focus on others you ask? You will find that there is a power in assisting others that reciprocates and helps you to feel meaning. In this simple way, you are advancing the healing of your own heart, mind, and soul. You can start the process of alleviating both yourself and others however, by developing a steady prayer life. Focusing on others is something that pleases the Lord. When a person focuses on others, God then helps a person with private and particular issues in a mysterious fashion. Your gratitude and outlook on life then soars to another height. The devil will try and keep this from happening and is why a consistent prayer life protects you from much of this.

You have to do whatever it takes to develop a consistent or at least constant daily prayer routine

Does prayer come easy or is it difficult? Sometimes we need to exceedingly apply ourselves and get to a place where we can focus and have quiet. Sometimes a brief prayer to God asking Him to help you properly pray, or to help you know what to pray is a vital starting point. When you start to develop a steady prayer life, begin with fifteen minutes in the both the morning and evening. A routine will naturally develop much like other habits. From there, as time moves forward, prayer gets to be a recreation that you look forward to and understand the dire need for each day. Asking God to help both yourself and others with simple words from the heart are all He wants and expects. You have to be committed and loyal to yourself in the beginning and get yourself accustomed to your prayer pattern.

The time you dedicate to Him in prayer will slowly increase because there will be a desire, a yearning to sit down and spend time alone with Him in your thoughts. We will do an end around again on this, but it is important to arrive on your own the fact that a relationship with Jesus is indispensable. I stated that this comes first by prayer and then working into doing things for yourself and others. This takes time and discipline to make time to pray. Without prayer however, a person cannot gain spiritual headway. The ultimate prayer in this life is the Holy Mass followed by being able to spend time with our Lord in Eucharistic Adoration. If a person can start to attend more masses, this amplifies and elevates the prayer life and the graces that come with it exponentially. This is a reality that we can discuss further, but both are topics for other books. It is important for the reader to consider going to and starting to spend time with our Lord in Eucharistic Adoration. You do not have to be any denomination, but you will only find it in a Catholic Church when the Blessed Sacrament, Jesus Himself, is exposed. Why more people do not avail themselves to these great graces speaks to how confused and off-track the world and society are at this point in history. Get yourself there, and get to mass, and find your world changing for the positive in an accelerated fast-tracked time period. It is important for the reader to at least hear about these spiritual necessities for now, and in time, God willing, they will be able to become our "go to" on earth.

You are valued enough to become an adopted son and daughter of Kingly royalty. Let that sink in!

We discussed that everyone has value in God's eyes. Your worth is beyond reasoning in the perception of our God. It is common not to be convinced of this truth. The evil one wants you to believe the exact opposite. It is another fallacy that he wants us to believe so our relationship with God is hindered or blocked. Think of someone who you really get along with and appreciate. This person has value in your eyes because you truly treasure their character, personality, or reciprocating friendship. Now amplify this cherished relationship when you start to fathom that God wants to be with us. He is enamored with His creation in us and relishes in the idea of being with us forever.

We are proud of things we make well. Why would it be any different for God our Creator? The truth is that we are well made by God. God does not poorly make anything, and therefore we are wonderfully made. We have this thing called an eternal soul that makes us invaluable to God. We become His children when we choose to do His will.

Consider what St. Paul tells this Galatian community. *"But when the fullness of time had come, God sent his Son, born of a woman, born under the law, in order to redeem those who were under the law, so that we might receive adoption as children. And because you are children, God has sent the Spirit of his Son into our hearts, crying, 'Abba! Father!' So you are no longer a slave but a child, and if a child then also an heir, through God"* (Galatians 4: 4-7). When you talk about being an heir, it means you have something to inherit. That something is heaven and all that is in it! A person has to claim it with love for God in return. A person has to claim all that which comes with this adoption. For now, that also means that we claim suffering and sacrifice as being a brother and sister to Jesus and progressing towards our eternal reward.

Serving God overall

Being created by God and for God has enormous merit and needs repeating to the reader. God would not have created you if He did not have a plan for your life. If He did not love you, then why create you? We cannot weigh worldly worth to what our lives mean to God. This is why we must respect life for both those not born yet and the elderly who sometimes may not be able to manifest physical health in their remaining years. It is God who should ultimately be the one who then also takes life back to Him through earthly death. We cannot pretend to play God because taking and making life is not for us to decide. We simply need to focus on loving, respecting, and serving life. He gives us love, care, and relationship especially with one another. It is certainly not unimaginable that God craves our attention and love in return. If we are honest, we would see that we need to spend time back with God for our relationship to continue to grow. The good news is that when we seek Him, we find Him in abundance!

Our lives are of value also to others whom we encounter. Those we live with and interact with should find significance in our relationship and vice versa. Even if we only know a few people or are close to only a small number of individuals, we fill an important aspect in their lives too. This is why we need to serve God by asking Him what He wants of us. Serving and helping others is one form of purpose in our lives. Through prayer, these notions and impressions come into our thoughts. These come to us when we try and discern what He is requesting from us. These perceptions then are implored upon to our Lord that assist us to be conclusive and certain.

Prayer too then provides purpose. It pleases God that we are trying to do what He expects. He summons us to become His children, and thus become patterned after His Son Jesus who is truly perfect in all things. In other words, we are called to be Christ like or Christians. St.

Paul says this of the marks of the true Christian. *"Let love be genuine; hate what is evil, hold fast to what is good; love one another with mutual affection; outdo one another in showing honor. Do not lag in zeal, be ardent in the spirit, serve the Lord. Rejoice in hope, be patient in suffering; persevere in prayer. Contribute to the needs of the saints; extend hospitality to strangers"* (Romans 12: 9-13)

For some it is overly burdensome to demonstrate hospitality to strangers. In a society that does not promote or commonly teach that there is intrinsic worth in living a concerned and compassionate lifestyle, people have to be taught to be attentive and unselfish toward others. Have you noticed that in larger cities, you can wave and say "Hi" to people and they will not even acknowledge you. It is counter to the way we are supposed to interact with one another. In other parts of the world, a smile and a wave are a normal means of showing cordial demeanor. I too admit it is challenging to be kind and patient one hundred percent of the time. It is, however, one way we serve the Lord when we engage in inconvenient and problematic situations that others confront.

In fact, it can be arduous and tiring to serve, but there is much grace that comes from interactions with those less fortunate than us. I am not referring to always providing physically or financially, but often just having a conversation or reaching out to those who may be chronically annoying or those in need of attention. These interactions can really help out others, and it teaches us the ways of virtue again.

Whatever is thorny and tough to undertake, a person can learn to be patient and train for how to overcome as St. Paul eludes. Through time and prayer however, one can discern the will of God in their lives and become that red cedar, that regal tree that we discussed earlier. We strive to become that solid and sound person because we attract other by demonstrating these traits. Others want to be around us and live the same type of lifestyle and traits. These honorable and distinctive traits are then recognized of us in heaven as well. Yes, we take these Christ-like character traits with us to heaven.

Practicing much virtue and doing good often become honors we will carry with us forever. God gives us the opportunities to have a high place of distinction in heaven. These are truths for another discussion, but again the reader needs to have these seeds planted to return to and learn further at a more appropriate season in their journey. Practicing prayer and forming virtuous acts take time. However, practicing these good deeds and virtues help oneself continue day to day. Eventually, one will recognize the value in what he or she's life and actions really mean in the big picture of eternity.

Starting to define Virtue

It is time to scrutinize and contemplate what it means to have perseverance, endurance, and strength. Were you ever outright taught in school that these virtues were important? Sometimes we hear things like "no pain no gain" or other slogans. Were we provided true examples of those individuals pushing through challenges? This is where learning about the saints' lives becomes invaluably important.

Were we taught that complaining is not a great practice to make into habit? It seems it is a norm of the environment and culture we live in to complain and balk. Were you ever even educated to know what virtues were? Well, it is time to ponder and look at our Lord's example for these and other highly righteous features that can bring us purpose.

Remember that we want to strive to provide meaning for our lives. Anything we can do to expand this meaningful state of mind is desirable and an advantage for us. Sometimes it helps us to get to witness or hear of how these virtues are presented. We can then replicate and elaborate upon these virtues in our own personal setting whatever that might be.

We will get into exact definitions shortly, but what is virtue first of all? Liam Brooks provides for us a great definition for virtue in general.

In his book *Catholic Devotions for Men,* pg. 70, he says, "*Virtue is the habitual inclination to do good. It is not a one-time act but a way of living-a constant pursuit of moral excellence that shapes our thoughts, actions, and decisions. The Catholic Church teaches that virtue is the foundation of a well-lived life, and that virtues are not just moral habits but reflections of the grace and love of God.*" I found that this definition exemplifies that aspect that is trying to be presented in this book, that virtue, especially lived out and developed upon the examples of Jesus Christ and His saints will provide that moral compass on doing the will of God the Father. This in turn therefore will help us discover our purpose towards heaven. Mr. Brooks edifies this and confirms this very sentiment. *Jesus Christ is the model of every virtue, and as men and women who follow him, we are called to imitate His virtues in our own lives* (pg. 70). St. Peter sheds light on this whole concept as well when he points out, "*To this you were called, because Christ suffered for you, leaving you an example, that you should follow in His steps" (1 Peter 2:21).*

As time goes on, it is intended the reader will go on to further study the four cardinal virtues. These include: prudence, justice, fortitude, (we are studying this somewhat now in strength when speaking of courage), and temperance. Learning the virtues of endurance, perseverance, and strength will build a spiritual and mental foundation coupled with the theological virtues of faith, hope and charity that we touch on in subsequent chapters.

Being cognizant of forming virtue

It is the intent to get the reader to be cognizant of and start to recognize and focus on the concepts of forming virtue. It is an obvious fact that most of us were not raised with any regularity in seeking such virtue, nor were we educated that these virtues are cornerstone to developing a formidable mental and spiritual structure. Our culture simply does not emphasize that these virtues need to be ingrained in our children with any great impetus. Therefore, we find our culture lacking and having to be re-educated in the value of virtue. We find that society suffers and does not even recognize that it needs its Creator.

What do these virtues mean to you? While they may seem to be intangible, they are actually tangible as well when people practice and demonstrate these in their lives. Do you see yourself already practicing these merit bearing assets? They are truly assets in the sense that there are graces derived from performing and intentionally committing these upright moral actions. The virtue bearer and the person served by the virtuous action mutually benefit. Both the hear- and-now and our futures will benefit from working hard to practice these virtues.

God rewards us with many blessings for doing the right things. Being righteous is Godly. He knows that the times we live in tempt us to be immoral, corrupt, or just plain lazy. These specific three virtues, strength, perseverance, and endurance are very important to surviving in the times we live.

Our world is changing fast and its necessary to be able to adapt. This can include dealing with complications and engaging in sufferings and sacrifice. These are not new concepts. All the saints in heaven got there by pushing through distress and woe. They asked God for His help. The object is to flourish and live a life of continual growth and development. The growth cannot come without burgeoning these virtues. However, a person has to either be taught or have a good example of what each means. When we get to the lives of the saints and the stories of Jesus these virtues become apparent because they are repeatedly demonstrated. In this case, actions truly speak louder than words. Like the old adage, "a picture is worth a thousand words", we will witness some of pictures these saints portrayed.

When one humbly accepts Jesus's invite to continually ask Him for help, one verily comes to a fuller understanding of why overcoming current troubles, problems, and challenges are something achievable.

Jesus wants us to ask for big things. He wants us to hold out a big cup for Him to fill for us. When we realize this, it is then that a glimmer of hope arises, or dare I say, that faith surges.

This hope arises from prayer and the knowledge one acquires the day that it hits home that none of a person's troubles are bigger than God. In other words, nothing is impossible for God! Sometimes a miracle can happen and God outright solves your issue. Hallelujah! And thanks be to God when that happens! For the other times when He is developing your character, He expects you to utilize these virtues of strength, perseverance, and endurance along with His grace to get you through the issue. He helps you when you help yourself. Sometimes requests are not answered quickly or automatically. Some come at the eleventh hour and fifty-ninth minute! These are the times our faith is tested, when we find ourselves in the middle of God testing our trust in Him.

Do you know why things are not always a miracle or automatically answered? Why things are not always immediately resolved? Often our prayers are not answered in the way we hope they will be answered. It is because God wants you to be like Jesus. What does this really mean?

Jesus's Glory is in His Cross and that equals suffering for a major cause, (You and me)

Jesus's qualities are what God loves. We know this from sacred scripture when God speaks of Jesus after the transfiguration on Mount Tabor. The transfiguration is where Jesus was shown to a few of the apostles in His glory. Those apostles, Peter, James and John, were part of a supernatural experience. They were told not to report the experience until after Jesus died. It is on this mountain where God the Father said of Jesus to the apostles, *"This is my Son, my Chosen, listen to him!"*. (Luke 9:35). Jesus had to suffer because of His glory. Jesus had not yet experienced suffering and thus His glory was not to be revealed until after His death. Do you know what the glory of Jesus is? It is His Cross. Yes, Jesus suffered and died on the Cross, but it is His glory. It is what our Lord is known for. He took it upon Himself to suffer for our sins. It is what He did that made Him so great of a Savior!

God restored Him and Jesus was resurrected from death and in this way, God beat death and sin. He won against the evil one for time and eternity. We too have to have the same glory, and God allows us to have these "crosses" in our lives from time to time. We also suffer, but this suffering is converted into our glory as well.

This is where we develop our ability to over-come the cross with the virtues and graces from God. It is why these virtues are so important to acquire, so we can be like Jesus and demonstrate the right to be called adopted sons and daughters of Jesus. Ask the Holy Spirit to make this clearer to you, and your will receive this insight. Ask for the grace to endure your crosses and bear them with joy. This suffering has eternal weight and worth. Read more of the lives of the saints and this will become a common theme.

So, let us get the definition of each virtue so we can process each meaning in our minds. As discussed, using these virtues will help you get through the present crisis, trends, challenges and problems you encounter. What do each of these virtues truly mean? One also needs to know the opposite of each virtue. Knowing the opposite of each virtue will help crystalize what each virtue is not, and therefore help us emulate and properly acquire each.

So, what is the definition of perseverance? *Perseverance*—is a continued effort to do or achieve something despite difficulties, failure, or opposition. This is the "keep on, keeping on" virtue. This is one we develop in our inner will. We talk to ourselves and make ourselves tough enough mentally to continue for as long as we need to. For anyone who is familiar with the Rocky movies, or a Rocky Balboa fan, it's the "Eye of the Tiger" type mindset that keeps one mentally fortified.

The opposite of perseverance than is apathy and indifference, and reluctancy, wavering, and hesitation. While we might experience these in our lives, we know that these do not move us forward, nor do they help us build on our strength and endurance. (Wordhippo.com)

What is the definition of endurance? *Endurance*—is the ability to withstand hardship or adversity. Especially: the ability to sustain a prolonged stressful effort or activity. This is more of the physical and mental ability to withstand the "wear and tear" of the longevity of something that we are experiencing. I personally believe the more perseverance one possesses, the better one's endurance. Endurance goes with strength such that there has to be the ability to endure first and strength is that ability. What endurance is not....It is not ceasing, stopping, or fatiguing to the point of closing down. This is an important distinction. While one can become weary and fatigue, it is not letting this fatigue overcome us or make us quit.

What is the definition of *strength*? While strength has multiple meanings as a noun, in this instance *Strength*—is the emotional, physical, or mental qualities necessary in dealing with situations or events that are distressing or difficult. I would argue that strength has much to do with one's physical condition and overall health of mind and body first and foremost. Strength needs to be built up and formed before one can persevere and/or endure. It is analogous to and a derivative of the virtue of fortitude. Fortitude can be substituted as a virtue in some of our examples when speaking of courage. We will come to cover this later on. It is imperative to develop strength through proper prayer by maintaining one's body and mind. You need proper rest and good nutrition for physical strength. On the spiritual and mental side of developing strength, one requires quiet time with God. One also has to develop spiritual strength to overcome evil. What is the opposite of strength then? The opposite of strength than is weakness, unsteadiness, and having paralyzing fear. We understand that these are most often negative in connotations, and therefore we try and develop our strength and fortitude. All these virtues are tied together and are attributes that help us persist and remain alive. They are God given. Thank you, Lord for all the good things you have provided for us in our lives, and for our purpose!

If you find yourself lacking in any of these virtues do not lose hope. This writing goes on to help provide examples and ideas for you to use to bolster these virtues. The more you ask God to help you gain these virtues the more virtue you will receive.

Call on the Holy Spirit to help us

At some point in life, perhaps a few years after the age of reason or early in the teen years, I recall trying to determine the purpose of why we were placed here in this human condition. What purpose was there for us being here? Why were we living life in the first place? Obviously, this is not only a difficult concept to answer for many reasons as a younger person, but also as an adult. Pondering our purpose naturally leads to many additional questions. It is when we start to experience thoughts of doubt and fear that we need to recognize that these are not of God. It has to be repeated that one should then call on God to remove the fear and doubt and pray for clarity and more trust in Him. It will for sure come. The Holy Spirit will develop these virtues in us if we ask Him to. *"By living out these virtues, we become the men God has called us to be – men of strength, character, and integrity." (Phillipians 2:13).*

In the younger years, while trying to formulate faith in God with prayer and trust in our educators, it was few and far between that teachers presented this information. Either as kids we did not know enough to ask regarding our purpose, or that everyone was focused on what type of education or career they were honing in on. Many of our schools and educators, even in a Catholic setting, dropped the ball on forming the youth towards purpose. Retrospectively speaking and encouraged by what I see today in the up-and-coming youth, I can say that there was a lack of Eucharistic belief and prayer before the Eucharistic Lord. It is only now that there is a movement to restore belief in our Lord Jesus in the Eucharist. Let us consider this reality, especially for those who may not understand that our Lord is present in the Eucharist during each Mass that is celebrated in the Catholic tradition. It's a huge deal!

As time has passed over the twentieth century, society fell away from God and was thus left to fend on its own. This had devastating repercussions in our country and over the world. Many educators failed to help people see the reason for our existence because we strayed from God, and eventually did not know Him. Relativism did not have room for God and abandoned faith in our Creator. The Catholic Religious sisters used to teach the Baltimore Catechism. This was the basics of the Catholic faith. There were some hard questions answered very easily by our Catholic faith that has progressed over two thousand years. We have just strayed away and went from winning the fight against evil, to taking the easy way out and being slothful with our existence as a culture and society.

Come to a realization by trusting in a mystery that will forever change your perspective and focus

Along with laziness, our hearts have grown cold and there are high percentages of people not believing in God. A big percentage of Catholics do not even believe in the crux of their faith, that Jesus is truly present in the Eucharist at the celebration of the Holy Mass. For those not Catholic, and those not formed well in the faith, Catholics believe that Jesus, after the Last Supper, instituted His priesthood to his Apostles, and performed the first Mass. Mass is the ceremony that continues the sacrifice of Christ on the Cross. It is here that Jesus allows Himself to be given to those who "assist" or participate in this celebration. Jesus gave His priests the ability to say Eucharistic prayers, "prayers of Thanksgiving" to change regular bread and wine to His true body and blood. It is referred to as Transubstantiation. While the scope of this book is not intended to cover this in full, one should dive further into this definition and understand this more. Please see the Catechism of the Catholic Church pgs.1373-77.

This sometimes throws people "off kilter" when they cannot get past this mystical miracle, but suffice it to say this is truth at its heart. Jesus said at the institution of the Lord's Supper at the Last Supper, *"Then he took a loaf of bread, and when he had given thanks, he broke it and gave it to them, saying, 'This is my body, which is given for you. Do this in remembrance of me. And he did the same with the cup after supper, saying, 'This cup that is poured out for your is the new covenant in my blood"* (Luke 22 verses 19-20).

Some have a most difficult time believing that Jesus is truly present in the Eucharist after the priest's consecrating words at that point in the mass prayer because it appears to be just bread in the host. They cannot get past the fact that mere prayers said by a true Catholic priest transforms this bread and wine into the Body and Blood of our Lord. The truth is that this has kept the Catholic Church going for over two thousand years. The Church realizes its existence lies in celebrating the Holy Mass and actually receiving Jesus in body, blood, soul, and divinity. Very few of the 8 billion of us on earth now really believe this to be true.

The devil has us right where he wants us when we do not have the faith that this is genuine and authentic in full. He knows that if he can persuade people to doubt, then he has the upper hand. It is not until you believe in this existential fact that you will be able to achieve your full purpose. This is another important factual point that one needs to study more. However, this helps put the entire topic into a framework for understanding purpose. I can understand how this might seem impossible, but do not forget there is a supernatural element that exists, and in this case it's the most important supernatural concept you can believe in. There are many miracles that prove this is true if you are doubting. You can research the authenticity of these miracles. In the end, you have to take that leap of faith in believing and you will be blessed remarkably for your belief.

As stated, this reality that Jesus is absolutely present at every mass said around the world each day, makes for the non-believer an impossibility to continue in a fullness of faith. Fullness of faith is what we are talking about when we seek true purpose. Pride and doubt can do irrevocable damage if there is not repentance of one's arrogance and disbelief. There are few other explanations for reasons why people have lost the desire to know God. Remember the whole purpose thing? To know, love, and serve God is the axis for our existence? Trust your gut on this and your conscience will tell you that Jesus comes to us in the Holy Eucharist. He promised He would never leave us, and this is His way of being truly present for us when we need Him. *"And remember, I am with you always to the end of the age"* (Matthew 28:20).

Making Jesus a priority will put you on a fast track to purpose

We need to make Jesus a priority, and our ultimate significance. He says it Himself that we need to love Him above all things. *"Whoever loves father or mother more than me is not worthy of me, and whoever loves son or daughter more than me is not worthy of me; and whoever does not take up the cross and follow me is not worthy of me. (*Matthew 10 37-38). Have you read the stories of World War II soldiers and spies who only had a few weeks and or days to learn how to prepare for their next major mission? They had to get to the point and get good at speaking languages, learning codes, and delivering plans that shaped the defeat of the Axis powers. They had to be disciplined and courageous and get to the point. The same with us. There is no time left in one's life to debate these truths. Time is ticking and one needs to "get right" with what God expects. Everyone needs to be reminded of our own "term limit" . *"Keep awake therefore, for you do not know on what day your Lord is coming"* (Matthew 24, 42). We want to be spiritually ready with good deeds in hand. He will never force us to follow Him, but if we continuously reject Him, we do so at our own eternal risk.

The Baltimore Catechism, (the solid catechism that boosted the Catholic Church forward in the United States in the mid- 1800's) is something not regularly taught anymore. It is, however, one of the bedrocks I believe that helped form young people's faith. When students studied and were taught by these simple standards of the faith the simple truths were presented in matter-of-fact form. In other words, one did not have to guess. I recommend picking up this direct instructional and allow its straightforward simplicity to brilliantly enlighten you. You will be on the receiving side of great foundational faith instruction. Instruction that guides towards purpose. (The New Saint Joseph Baltimore Catechism, Official Revised Edition, 1964, by Fr. Bennet Kelly).

Simplicity wins the day

The catechism gives us simple straight forward truths that help establish rationale for our faith. When studying the first lesson, question number six inquires, "*Why did God make us*?" The response comes back with a profoundly simple answer. *"God made me to know Him, to love Him, and to serve Him in this world, and to be happy with Him forever in heaven."* (Baltimore Catechism, 1885). So far, we have talked about learning to love God, and we are also dabbling with the concept of the various ways we can serve Him.

The more prominent question is getting to know him, and this only comes with studying Him in holy scripture, praying for the grace to know Him, and being given that very grace. The "*...be happy with Him forever in heaven*" is the culmination of knowing, loving and serving Him in this life. Hopefully some of these truths offered to the reader are starting to advance the perception of our purpose?

There are many who are asking this question right now as to what purpose do their lives have in the big picture of both universe and time. Why were they given life, and to whom does it matter? Why were we chosen to live in this exact moment of history? What part of the puzzle does my life's "piece" fit into. It is almost always easier to know *why* we are doing something as this gives purpose to processes and missions.

Therefore, while there is value in answering the larger "Why" questions in most situations, the struggle comes to believe the truth about the why. Our "Why" originates from the fact that God created us in our mother's womb to someday be with Him for eternity. He establishes our lives here on earth after forming us, and we are to learn about Him and decide to live our lives ultimately for Him. We are to give witness to His glorious and merciful nature towards we, His creation.

Before getting too in-depth with our contemplation on life's purpose, (and without taking too much of a tangent) people have to understand that there is both God our Creator, who is all good and loving, but there is also an evil force, an evil one (Satan, Lucifer, the devil). The devil, while not anywhere close to being as powerful as our God, still has permission to tempt humans for their mental, spiritual, and physical faithfulness to God and His laws. This is one of those truths and concepts I am telling the reader to trust me on. There are all these subtopics that we are uncovering in which it is your job to get the basics for now, and then go back and study more of these elements that effect your lives.

God created us. He also created Lucifer (and the other fallen angels). Lucifer which means, "Bearer of the Light" was supposedly a very prominent angel at one point. We know however, that Lucifer rebelled in Heaven when put to the test. It is said that Lucifer was given the choice to serve God, but rather wanted to make himself God. The angels were all given this option to follow God or believe that they could be God. One third of the angels failed the test and were ousted from Heaven by St. Michael the Archangel. They had one chance to pass the test, and that was choosing to follow God. Because these fallen angels knew the right answer but chose against God, they were removed and allowed to be separated from God forever by their own volition. (Revelations 12:7-9).

You and I have the same sort of test. The test, however, is lifelong because of our human nature. We have our entire lives until our last breath to pass the test. The difference is we are not solely spirits like the angels who knew right and wrong from their beginning. We are spirit and flesh with a soul and have weaknesses with our strengths. When we fail at serving God and seek repentance and pick ourselves up and keep trying to do what God wills and wants for us, we are passing that test. We seek forgiveness and it is given to us through the Sacrament of Reconciliation. (This is another aspect of living a Catholic life and a separate topic that one needs to further research, but nonetheless an absolute truth). The Sacrament of Reconciliation we will speak about further, but for those who wish to know more, it can be referenced in the Catechism of the Catholic Church (pgs. 980, 1423).

We live life trying to become holy and serving God. This is our test and we must use virtue and belief in God to pass it. The Lord knows us and will help us pass the test if we only show that we love Him and Him alone as God. The Old Testament, the book of Jeremiah says this, "*Before I formed you in the womb, I knew you, and before you were born I consecrated you;*" (Jeremiah 1:5). God must have known our souls and our spirit even before we were "*wonderfully made*" (Psalm 139 verse 14). This is another reason to want to resume a homecoming with Him.

My job is to introduce to you, or remind you of, or prompt you to the basics regarding your purpose. This involves getting on track, or back on track following Jesus. This concept of evil is nothing to dismiss as folly. It is also important on the other end of the spectrum to not over pursue an interest in evil, because the devil is infinitely smaller and insignificant in comparison to our God. The problem comes when people believe that age old lie that Satan wants people to believe. The belief that he, the devil, does not exist!

This foolishness plagues many people. Their imprudence and lack of wisdom on the topic can lead them to their own demise. It is as simple as that. We need to learn how to ask for God's protection. God gives us the grace to foil the devil's plan and tricks. We need to learn how to walk away from temptations, and learn that the devil sets traps for our souls. We can call on the name of Jesus to help us anytime we are being attacked by the devil or his minions. We also can ask the Holy Angels to come to our assistance and fend off attacks and temptations.

For an interesting real-life story on the subject, please reference the life of Zachary King, Satanist turned Catholic, a YouTube presentation. It will knock your socks off. After listening to this true story, one should feel pretty compelled to take seriously this topic. It was because of Jesus's mother our Blessed Saintly Mother Mary, that she helped rescue Zach back to Jesus. Zach is eternally grateful to our Blessed Mother for her intervention in his life. Take time to look into this story. It is compelling to say the least.

We also must ask our Blessed Mother to protect us from Satan. This is non-negotiable because he hates Her. He cannot handle the prayer of the Hail Mary. He knows that in God's due time, our Blessed Mother "crushes" his head. She as destined by God, ushers in the reign of Jesus her son. It is called the Reign of the Immaculate Heart of Mary and Sacred Heart of Jesus. This then brings to us the Era of Peace.

I have always wondered why God allows evil, or Satan to wreak havoc on humanity? Really? What does God owe him other than to lock him away forever and prevent him from hurting us. Yes, there is a Hell and that I want to make it abundantly clear. This is not where we want our final dwelling place to be. We ultimately want to avoid this physical and spiritual place of separation from God. It is a place that only allows for a contemptuous state of mind that is totally void of God. Those that find themselves there are miserable and in perpetual anguish because they chose that for themselves. Sounds awful does in not?

There are many mystics that will provide a testimony for our sake so we ultimately do not end up in this horrendous place of torment. Let it be enough for now to say that God does not choose us to wind up in Hell, but we ultimately can choose this destination directly or indirectly by not loving God. Not loving God can come in many forms and therefore we need to learn how to foster the three virtues that we continue to discuss. By expounding on perseverance, endurance and asking for the grace of more strength, we become like Jesus. By becoming like Jesus, we reflect and exude goodness all around.

For both those who have faith and no faith, the question as to what is the purpose of life is infinitely daunting with the pressures the evil one can unexceptionally place on the human mind. If one searches interiorly and is honest about what comes into one's thoughts, one knows and senses that there is a higher reality. If you happen to have any doubts as to God's existence, (an assured temptation from the evil one, I might add), just ask your guardian angel to enlighten your consciousness. Ask the Holy Spirit to fill you with knowledge. Knowledge is one of the seven gifts of the Holy Spirit, and one that He will provide you. And yes, you have a guardian angel. This is someone else with whom you need to build a relationship. This is another concept to trust me on, and take time to use other resources to learn more about angels and guardian angels. I recommend the book St. Michael and the Angels, by Tan Books 1977.

Speaking of angels, one also needs to learn of the protection of the Commander of the angelic armies, St. Michael. St. Michael is the one

God sends to defeat Satan. St. Michael is a stud of heavenly proportion and will come to our aid when called upon. Do some additional research, but understand that angels will help us get to our dwelling place. Remember to start with your guardian angel to first form a relationship. Guardian angels want to become our best friends. Finally, do not forget about all the friends we have in heaven already.

I write this book to you on the Feast of All Saints Day 2025. These "Friends in High Places", (as referred to by Patrick Madrid, Catholic Radio show host and overall expert on biblical interpretations and Catholic teachings), have the job of now helping those on earth become saints too. These real-life brothers and sisters of ours are waiting to help us with our requests and will be more than happy to intercede or ask God to grant our prayers. Remember, these saints were here before us and understand our struggles.

Some would say we feel yearnings and urges in our souls to want to be with God. This is certainly a supernatural longing and one that is quite real. Our souls were created to live eternally. Each of our souls will be judged based on the decisions made in life either to do good or to do evil. God wants us to do good. Part and parcel of this is honoring him and living our lives for Him first and foremost and then for our family, country, and others in this type of hierarchy. He wants us to reflect His love and to do good. This is referred to as being righteous.

Yes, we are called to love God who created us. Jesus is love itself and He calls to each and every one of us. If one quiets and stills the soul, blocking out extraneous interferences, there is the desire not to be of this earth, but in a place of peace, with no stress whatsoever. The true meaning of rest and leisure is being immersed in prayer and worship. There is an innate need to be without pain, without discouragement, without worry, and that is part of the reason we take on the constant barrage of challenges and issues here and now, face to face with worldly living. God is this peace we so desperately seek.

Again, some people through no fault of their own, were not introduced to a faith, nor experienced the Good News of the Gospel of Jesus. If a person was simply culturized into the false lure and draw of money, power, prestige, and comfort, it is no wonder that theses attractions are steadfastly sought after as an end all to happiness. Realize that these false exhilarations can be the enticement to a fabricated purpose . It is not that these things are evil in and of themselves, but they eventually let you down and leave you empty. After someone accumulates all of these, one is still not satisfied and is looking for other ways to be fulfilled. It is true. The deceitfulness progresses from one artificial enticement to the next. None retain happiness or joy. The happiness is fleeting and superficially shallow. When looking at the world we live in, its apparent we have no lasting joy. It is painfully reflected in the way we treat one another each day.

With the idea that we will one day be examined for how we live our lives, it behooves us immensely to try and do good all the days of our lives. Doing good and becoming simple for Jesus gives us lasting joy and peace. This joy is continuous when we do not focus on ourselves. Rather by serving God simply and not overcomplicating our service we gain this joy and peace. Our service can, but does not have to be great deeds. Small acts of kindness can make one a great saint. "*Fear God, and keep his commandments; for that is the whole duty of everyone. For God will bring every deed into judgement, including every secret thing, whether good or evil*" (Ecclesiastes 12 :13-14). This verse is not meant to make one fearful of God, however the reality is that time is urgent and that good deeds and faith are required each day of one's life.

Commit to memory that one needs to grow in knowing God each day as this will strengthen faith. When faith becomes strong, so will the desire to know God become more plentiful. So, be patient and take a month or two to ask God each day to help you see the purpose in life. Then step out and make this short consecration each day, *"Jesus Christ my Lord and Savior, I consecrate this day my whole life and being and everything I have and do, to Your Kingship. In so doing, I consecrate myself to God the Father and the Holy Spirit. Please protect myself and my family from evil. Allow me to serve you this day and always. Take me to your Father's House one day after I have completed the tasks that your plan calls for me to complete. I love you with my whole mind, soul and heart. Bless and cover my family and I this day with your Precious Blood. Amen."*

We touched on how the devil can tempt a person to strive for the acquisition of worldly things. While material tangibles and self-actualization intangibles can seem to gratify for a time, there is the need to offer oneself entirely to our all-powerful God. This is called consecration to God. It is important to do so daily. The above consecration reaffirms our allegiance to our God. It serves to solidify our desire to be with God each and every day. This consecration is actually shunning the worldly to reestablish your spiritual "Yes" each day to God. Your daily consecrations spotlight your intentions to get to that heavenly dwelling place. It starts to become your nucleus and center of your life the more you practice it.

Consider St. Francis De Sales's enthusiasm for being with God and rejecting the evil one. *"Hell, I detest you now and forevermore. I detest your torments and your pains. I detest your accursed wretched eternity. Above all, I detest the eternal blasphemies and maledictions that you eternally vomit forth against my God. I turn my heart and my soul toward you, O wonderous heaven, everlasting glory, and endless happiness, and choose my abiding place forever within your beauteous and sacred mansions and among your holy, longed-for tabernacles. O my God, I bless your mercy and accept the offer you are pleased to give to me. O Jesus, my Savior, I accept you everlasting love and hail the place and lodging you have purchased for me in this blessed Jerusalem".* (Francis De Sales, Introduction to the Devout Life, pg. 68).

Remember that our dedication to God will increase our desire to be with Him. St. Augustine of Hippo, states this concept most succinctly when he cries out to the Lord in one of the most quoted saint statements of all time when he says, "*Thou movest us to delight in praising Thee; for Thou has formed us for Thyself and our hearts are restless till they find rest in Thee. Lord, teach me to know and understand which of these should be first, to call on Thee or to praise Thee; and likewise, to know Thee, or to call upon Thee.* (Confessions 1, 1.5). St. Augustine, writing this about 1400 years earlier, backs up the Baltimore Catechism regarding the idea that God formed us for Himself.

Let us remind ourselves that many have had to ponder this purpose before us. One has to recall human origin history to find out our purpose. It is because the fall of our first parents Adam and Eve who God loved and made without original sin, that we find our world in disarray. In their disobedience to God (the devil tricked them in a bad way), they left us spiritually hindered and targets to the evil one. Since this sin produced in us a weakened condition, we find ourselves in a circumstance where we are required to get up each day and ultimately undertake what each day necessitates from us.

Because of this disobedience we needed to have a Savior, and God sent his only Son to help us out with a way to salvation. This Savior Jesus is the actual Word of God and Love himself. His sacrifice on the cross, while it gives us a means to salvation, does not mean we still do not have to persevere and endure many trials in order to demonstrate our worthiness of Him. We live in a sinful and fallen world and therefore had to have a Savior come to release us from the slavery of sin. Jesus's act of suffering on the cross was a redemptive act and allows us to get to the Kingdom of Heaven. Because heaven is a place without sin, and we are to be sinless citizens of this unimaginable yet real dimension, we need to have our sins forgiven. This comes again with the Sacrament of Reconciliation. Once we are provided this forgiveness in the sacrament, we feel mysteriously drawn and grateful to God who rules our world and heaven.

Remember too that Heaven is a very thrilling and intriguing place. We are told by St. Paul in his first book to the Corinthians, "*But, as it is written, 'What no eye has seen, nor ear heard, nor the human heart conceived what God has prepared for those who love him"* (Corinthians, 2,9). This is a yearning for God and being with him spiritually cannot be described in full.

For those of us Catholics, we continue to ruminate that the Catholic Church is the only Church founded and anchored with the apostles by Jesus Christ. We rely on its two-thousand-year history that has yet to be overcome. We look to the Catechism of the Catholic Church when it states the following regarding heaven, *"Heaven is the ultimate end and fulfillment of the deepest human longings, the state of supreme, definitive happiness. To live in heaven is 'to be with Christ'". The elect live 'in Christ', but they retain, or rather fund their true identity, their own name"* (1024, 1025, pg. 289-290, Catechism of the Catholic Church).

I think God is so excited to show us a better place that He created, that He is hurt when some of us choose to worship the opposite, and thus refuse His invite to this sublime and unspeakable place He created. Heaven it is said by mystics, has different colors, music, and scents. Imagine the prettiest places and most captivating spots on earth. He created these spots in heaven too. The point is that He can and has made an even more beautiful existence somewhere we have not yet visited. It is our jobs to follow Jesus there. How adventurous and breath taking this should be for us. How invigorating it should be to contemplate and want to be there forever.

In Summary

Let us summarize the many components we have included to consider in this chapter. In essence we are living this life to prove we are worthy to be with God. By evidencing our love, devotion and loyalty to Him and by following the life of Jesus Christ, we honor what he asks of us. He ultimately and definitively provides everything in giving

Himself to us. The Catechism of the Catholic Church states this about the purpose of life, "*By love, God revealed himself and gives himself to man. He has thus provided the definitive,* superabundant answer *to the questions that man asks himself about the meaning and purpose of his life*" (69, pg. 28).

It becomes our task then to discover as much about Him and ask Him each day to help us with the grace (divine assistance) to get to know Him. The concept of asking Him for this grace is referred to as prayer and is crucial to do this often and much. Loving Him is the key to all of the aforementioned, because He loved us first!

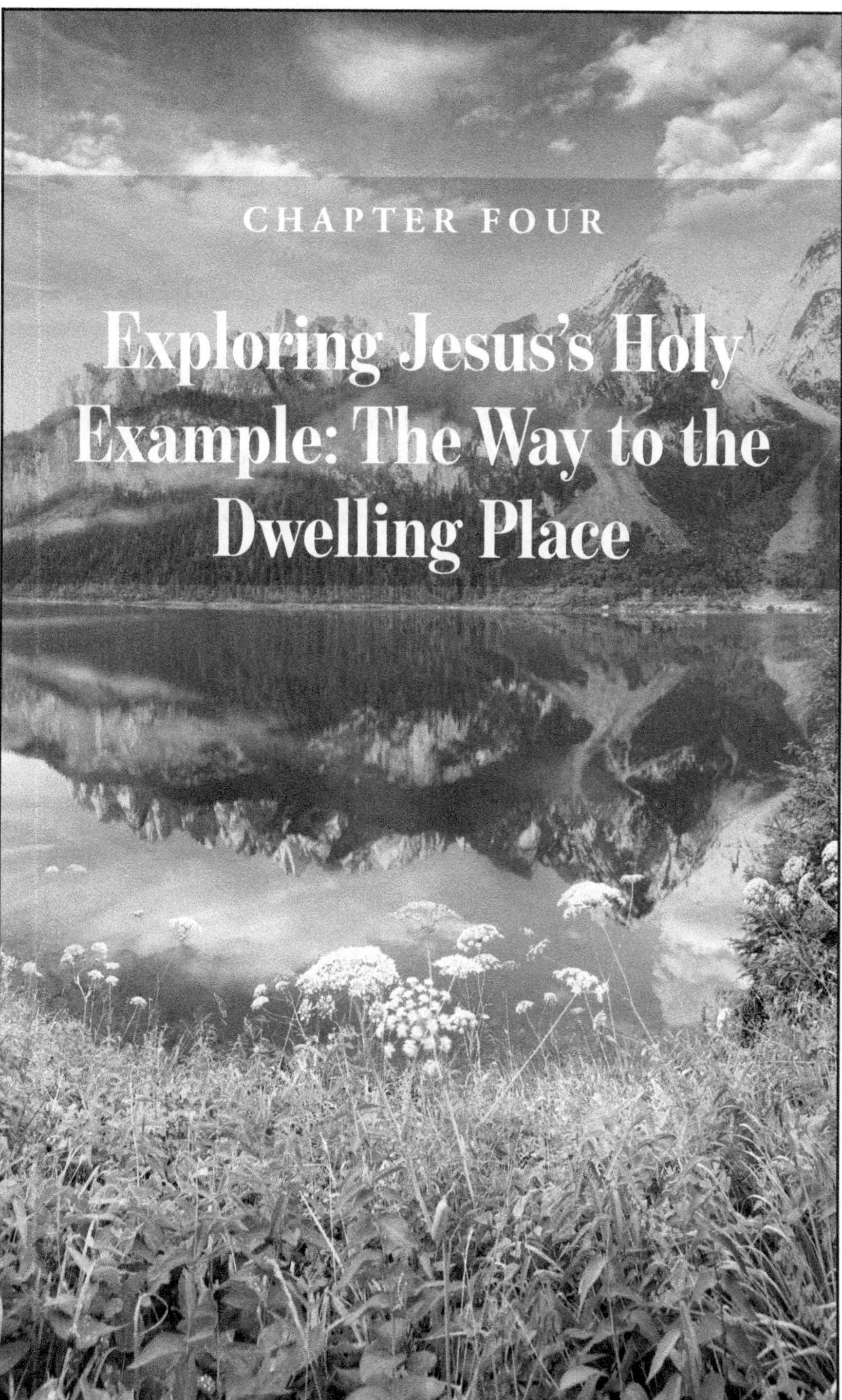

CHAPTER FOUR

Exploring Jesus's Holy Example: The Way to the Dwelling Place

Are you familiar with the four Synoptic Gospels? St. Matthew written circa 70 A.D., St. Mark, (thought perhaps to be an apprentice to St. Peter), St. Luke, physician and writer under the auspices of St. Paul, most likely the author of The Acts of the Apostles (a New Testament book as well), and St. John, (while not known for sure to be the author of the Gospel of St. John), it is most likely, in my humble opinion, "the beloved disciple", and author of the Letters of John in the New Testament. These four written Gospels are a culmination of the Good News of Jesus Christ.

If you happen to recall many of the stories that St. Matthew, St. Mark, St. Luke, and St. John provide for us with the Holy Spirit's inspiration, you might wish you could have had even more details about the events and situations presented at that time in history? Sometimes we are only provided with enough information to make a point, or give an example. An account or interview with the apostles themselves could have helped us know Jesus more. These stories were ultimately from the apostles or the Blessed Mother who handed them down.

I personally wish we could have learned more about Jesus's youth for example and perhaps the challenges that He had in that particular timeframe of His life on earth. What miracles might have He displayed in family life? I recall, however, the last words of the Gospel of St. John, *"But there are also many other things that Jesus did; if every one of them were written down, I suppose that the world itself could not contain the books that would be written"* (John 21, 25). I have many questions to ask our Lord someday regarding various ways he responded and acted. Why were there not more examples of the Holy Family's life together?

For example, why were there not more examples of the time Jesus, our Blessed Mother Mary, and St. Joseph spent together. Or, why were not more examples provided of Jesus's teen age and early twenties? It would be nice to know what He did in His spare time, or what hobbies He had. What did He do as a younger man that was interesting? One can be sure that he performed miracles that were probably not public, but "under the radar" just to help out people.

What if you grew up just a few houses down from Him and you played games and activities with Him as one of your friends? The examples we do have however, give us a clear representation of how grounded and focused Jesus was at all times. I believe it was because of this focused and resolute determination to do the will of His Father, that Jesus is able to give us the best examples possible for our own life applications. Let us consider some of these examples.

The strength our Savior provides is an extraordinary representation of really how strong he was mentally, physically, and spiritually. Some would comment, "*Of course he was strong and resilient, He was God!*", While they are not wrong, one cannot forget that Jesus's second nature was that of being human like us. (His first nature is that of being God as the second person of the Holy Trinity). I am paraphrasing the great biblical scholar Cale Clarke when I repeat, *Do not be fooled for a second that Jesus was not Divine from the beginning, many are the Old Testament prophecies that point to Jesus being the Messiah or Savior and both truly God and truly man* (Jesus 101, Relevant Radio Series). Do not be fooled like the Jehovah's witnesses that do not truly believe that Jesus is God. *"He became truly man while remaining truly God. Jesus Christ is true God and true man. During the first centuries, the Church had to defend and clarify this truth of faith against the heresies that falsified it"* (Catechism, 464, pg. 130).

While being both God and man, Jesus felt pain, became frustrated at times, and still was all knowing. He had to endure the ignorance of His apostles and peoples of the time, much like He endures our arrogance, pride, apathy and at times our lukewarmness. He endures us even during times when we reject Him outright. When was the last time you rejected His teachings based on your own selfishness? The Good News is, Jesus forgives us when we truly repent and seek out His love and friendship again. He does this through the Sacrament of Reconciliation of which we have previously discussed. It is so very important to hammer home the need to experience this Sacrament. Everyone needs the weight of their sins to be lifted off and feel the relief of being released from the burden and guilt.

He, Jesus Christ, exhibits His holy strength, perseverance and endurance in not only His life's narratives , but in the lives of others by the grace He provided them. Namely the grace in the lives of the Saints of the Catholic Church, but also other ordinary people we can relate to. These people were truly granted His special refinement and elegance in displaying degrees of these same virtues in contending with all that each withstood. If we are honest, we admit that none of us likes the idea of having to "bear our burdens", or "carry our crosses". Each of us has our own unique troubles to face and deal with.

We are instructed by Church teaching however, that it is in this life that one needs to suffer and sacrifice for the name of Jesus. How do we find purpose in our aches, pains and stresses? One has to realize that calling on the Holy name of Jesus helps us to begin to speak the "*Language of heaven*", (Smith, 2025). Asking Jesus to fight the fight for us is something He desires to take on for us. It is what He does and earnestly wants to help us with. He wants to help unsaddle burdens and not have to haul around our detrimental and draining loads. This should be an appealing and welcoming idea for us. We need to give Him the permission to help us out however we need assistance. Yes, it is correct that we need to give Jesus permission to take these worries from us, because God does not interfere with our free will. We need to surrender these obligations and stresses to Him and ask Him to completely take over.

Once we give Him this permission and truly step aside (this is the hard part because it requires true faith and trust), He can then intervene. God does not intrude upon our free will to decide to have Him in our lives. By allowing Him in to our interior mind, heart, and soul allows Him to heal us. He can then begin to provide for us this healing and intervention. We choose and love Him, and He restores and rebuilds.

Sometimes getting to the point where we almost entirely give up, is often the time we need to recognize it is time to surrender. It is usually after trying multiple ways to correct or fix something in our lives. When nothing seems to work, we are exhausted, angry, and defeated. Once we ask for the help, it comes sometimes at once, sometimes little by little, and sometimes it is necessary to continue praying and sacrificing.

It is when one worries and has little trust, however, that Jesus is reluctant to act. Jesus states in a particular prayer of Surrender that worry goes against this complete surrendering of ourselves (Surrender Novena, Fr. Dolindo). One needs to step back and get out of our own way and let God do His thing. *"But Moses said to the people, 'Do not be afraid, stand firm, and see the deliverance that the Lord will accomplish for you today; for the Egyptians whom you see today you shall never see again. The Lord will fight for you, and you have only to keep still"* Exodus 13-14). Sometimes the fight happens gradually, and instantaneously at other times. It is your choice to ask Him to help. Its then time to surrender fully and get out of the way and let Him resolve the issue. A copy of the link to this Novena is posted in the Appendix. (See Appendix A). I suggest that you become familiar now with this Novena. A Novena is a prayer that is often nine days in duration. It gives time for the praying individual to focus on the topic, and develops a short routine that I believe shows God you are serious about what you are asking for.

As mentioned above, this desire to spread a devotion to our Lord's Holy strength, perseverance and endurance was something I have felt for approximately the last 25 years. We know of Jesus's strength, but I as a cradle Catholic do not recall truly focusing on or worshiping Jesus for these remarkable attributes. Many authors, pastors, priests, touch on various aspects of how Jesus sacrifices Himself, but rarely do I hear or read about the virtues He displays in these sacrifices. Namely His strength of mind and body that He demonstrates to us. Also, Jesus demonstrates to us the perfect example of perseverance and endurance in many ways. Let us consider a few of these times in which He keenly expresses sense of these virtues. Keep in mind, these three virtues can be manifested in the physical, mental, and spiritual dimensions.

One of my favorite examples of strength is revealed when Jesus defended the woman caught in adultery. This is a moment beyond humbling and embarrassing for this poor woman. Can you think of a time you were exposed in front of others for something you were caught in the middle of doing? I know I can. I was caught saying a very choice explicative in the fourth grade, one of which I did not know the meaning, but rather that it was a forbidden word to speak as a child. I'd heard others saying this word and I thought it might sound mature to try it out. I said the particular word and soon after my aunt, grandmother, mother and whomever else were in the room went into crazed mob mode. They were going to insure this did not go without punishment. That did not go so well for me in the late nineteen seventies. I had to repent and then some! I had to look my father in the eye and tell him what I had said and why. I did not know why really. I thought it might be appropriate for the situation. The point is I had to ask for forgiveness and that is what we need to do to Jesus with our mistakes. He makes things right again between us and the Father. Jesus has the power to forgive sins and that is what He proved many times. He knows we make honest mistakes, and that our pride or inability to be humble put us in predicaments.

The Gospel of St. John Chapter 8, explains to us that the scribes and Pharisees brought Jesus a woman that was found to have committed adultery. They had absolutely no concern for this woman, but are trying to undermine what Jesus is going to say about this whole incident. They think they are laying a trap for Jesus. Sound somewhat evil already? The Jewish authorities are interested in ensnaring Jesus, and are coming for a way to ambush Him. The context of the story is such that these authorities want a way in which to accuse Jesus of not following the law of Moses (Mosaic Law). To put the circumstances into context, immediately before this incident, Jesus was already "under their skin" somewhat. They started to question and challenge His authority in preaching in the synagogues, healing paralyzed people, and refuting accusations of breaking Sabbath law and going to dinner with tax collectors and other outcasts (a shunned societal action of the time). Jesus displays His inner strength of compassion in not condemning this woman versus automatically following through on a Mosaic law that stated she needed to be stoned to death. He stood His ground and showed some backbone not allowing these bullies to intimidate Him.

This did not thrill the Jewish authorities because Jesus directly embarrasses them and beats them at their own game in His response. We hear them speak out in John 8:5, *"Now in the law Moses commanded us to stone such women. Now what do you say? They said this to test him, so that they might have some charge to bring against him."* What I really love about this passage is that Jesus is very confident in Himself and demonstrates this strength by not caving into the demands of these local authorities. He did not provide an answer at first, and that action alone showed the beginning of His strength. He had been bent down writing in the ground with his finger. On a side note, if you recall this story, did you ever wonder what it was he was writing? (My guess is that He maybe was writing their names on the ground that they might see He knew their names).

He eventually stood up since they kept questioning him, but He challenged them with this statement, "*Let anyone among you who is without sin be the first to throw a stone at her*" (John 8, 7). They all walk away we are told beginning with the elders. Most likely the elders caught on first. Probably because they were responsible for other stoning deaths in their time. In my estimate, they reflected on His words and were convicted in their hearts of their own past unforgiveness and condemnations. One can only speculate. Either way Jesus sent them packing.

Jesus controls the entire situation

Jesus demonstrates His strength in that He does not condemn when He, being God, could have done so otherwise. He rather chooses mercy. I love this! I think this is one of the most remarkable scenes of drama in the gospel according to John. *"Woman, where are they? Has no one condemned you? She said, "'No one, sir". And Jesus said, "Neither do I condemn you. Go your way, and from now on do not sin again"* (John 8: 10-11). Wow! Talk about a tone setter for these people that there is a new Sheriff in town named Jesus. He is taking evil head on unapologetically and without fear. I want Jesus in my corner! He shows Mercy because He is Mercy itself. I need more mercy Lord...

Can you take away from this gospel example any help in being able to stand firm in purpose and defend maybe yourself or others? Can you find purpose in showing mercy to others? Maybe, in your own way, you are the woman at the well? In this instance it is a good time to reflect and be silent. Maybe just pray to the Lord for His forgiveness and learn how to forgive oneself. You can get purpose and meaning back by forgiving yourself when needed. This can take some time however, but if you have ever had months and years of not being able to forgive yourself, then it is time to do so. God wants you to be forgiven. Remember that the devil wants to condemn you and tell you lies that make you believe that you are unworthy to be forgiven. Do not listen to these lies! Instead, run at top speed to Jesus when these thoughts come. Ask Him simply to come into the situation and help you make sense of the situation.

You must learn to forgive yourself

First seek the Lord by going to confession. For those of you not Catholic, a sincere and contrite heart will not be scorned it says in scripture. Your honest sorrow is acceptable to Jesus. If you do decide to convert to Catholicism and are able to go to the Sacrament of Reconciliation, you will praise God afterwards. Psalm 51 : 17 says this, "*The sacrifice acceptable to God is a broken spirit; a broken and contrite heart Oh God, you will not despise.*" He is looking to forgive us. You owe it to yourself to be able to forgive you. If Jesus can forgive you, there is no justification for you not to forgive yourself.

You learn from being disciplined. Most often you do not commit the same mistake going forward once you are truly sorry and understand that offending God is something you avoid at all costs. You live and learn from the mistake and fight temptation to repeat that same sin. The sacrament of Penance gives you grace to not sin further and is therefore very powerful. Spiritual liberation with bursting relief and joy is the way I can describe this blessing. A person honestly feels like there is a new lease on life.

Remember, Jesus is our example to follow. Remember, however, that we cannot fight a spiritual battle unless we use spiritual weapons. I have not emphasized this yet, but it is an important component to waging this invisible war. Remember that our fight is a spiritual fight with evil. The devil is a spiritual being. If we try and take him on as a human we will lose bigtime. This does not mean we should shy away from engaging him in this battle because we have Jesus and what He provides for us. He gives us spiritual weapons in reciting the rosary,

Eucharistic Adoration, blessed sacramentals, prayers, priestly blessings, a guardian angel, and Christ Himself in fighting the battle for us.

Recall that we can call on our guardian angels to help us out when pressed hard by evil. They are our spiritual protection and counter punch evil for us. When you find yourself pinned down by others who inadvertently or directly are looking for your ruin, call on the Holy Spirit for protection, call on your guardian angel to enlighten you on how to act. He being God, will give you the actions and words necessary to come to your own defense. Our angels are directed by God to oversee our safety, but we need to be willing to cooperate with them. We need to develop this personal best friend relationship.

Sidenote tangent: (For those readers not accustomed to the concept of going to a priest for the sacrament of Reconciliation (otherwise known as confession, or the Sacrament of Penance), I cannot overemphasize the spiritual sense of release and lightness that comes from having sins forgiven. The removal of the burden of carrying the inequities of our faults is true freedom.

The Sacrament of Penance, you have nothing to lose but the sin that binds you

I can tell you that the sacrament itself is supernatural experience, that, in and of itself, can give new meaning and purpose in experiencing deliverance from our offenses against God. I highly encourage all Catholics who have not experienced this sacrament in sometime to seek this sacrament and all its graces without any fear. You will not regret confronting your mistakes because it is both cathartic and unshackling. It invigorates one's spiritual life afterwards.

Again, there is nothing to be trepid or anxious about with the priest. There is nothing new under this solar system that these priests have not heard. Yet, people can be ashamed and feel self-resentment that prevents them from attending this beautiful sacrament. This is not uncommon. Reuniting oneself to the Lord, to His Church, is an absolute way of finding this purpose and meaning once more.

If you need to do something therapeutic and healing, do not hesitate to put yourself in front of Jesus in this Sacrament. The priest is in the place of Christ even though Christ is present. "*In persona Christi*" is the phrase regarding "*in the person of Christ*" which refers to the priest being in the place of Christ. Jesus's greatest attribute is His Mercy, and this gift is to be utilized. You cannot go wrong! I encourage you to look up local confession times at the parishes in your area. If these times do not work, a priest would be happy to set an appointment and meet with you to hear your confession. Its free!

How do you get to experience the Sacrament of Reconciliation and other Sacraments?

For those not Catholic, I encourage you to consider becoming Catechized in the Roman Catholic Church's faith, and being able to experience this forgiveness as an end component to the Order of Christian Initiation (OCIA). OCIA is the way one enters the Catholic Church. It is approximately 6-9 months in length. It consists of spiritual education (sometimes less, sometimes more) and catechesis (specific Church teachings and traditions). During this development time, your questions are answered about the faith. It is merely a learning timeframe that allows one to grow in understanding and ask questions before fully coming into the Church. While you can have your sins forgiven by being Baptized for the first time, this would be an additional way of experiencing forgiveness and starting a whole new journey to purpose-filled living. Jesus set it up this way for us, and gives Himself in the confessional with His priest. Do not fall for the old trap that says, *"I do not need to go to any human being for God to forgive my sins"*. This is a ploy again by the devil to keep you in a pride-filled state that simply perpetuates your condition. The sacrament is there for a reason and it is for you to encounter with nothing but humility and sorrow for your sins. Trust me on this. Do not be fooled into thinking that one can go without this grace. Jesus said this to Peter, *"And I tell you that you are Peter, and on this rock I will build my church, and the gates of Hades will not prevail against it. I will give you the keys of the kingdom of heaven, and whatever you bind on earth will be bound in heaven, and whatever you loose on earth will be loosed in heaven"* (Matthew 16:18-20).

If already baptized, yet not Catholic, I mentioned that one can begin OCIA. It is in this process that one "enters" the Church at the Easter Vigil, (the anticipatory Mass celebration the evening before the day of Easter, but "counts" as an Easter Mass celebration). Some parishes offer OCIA in the late summer and early fall too. One receives full admission to the Church at that Vigil Mass. During that Mass celebration, the catechumen (the candidate to come into the Church) typically receives either Eucharist (Holy Communion), and Confirmation (Receiving the Holy Spirit), but sometimes also Baptism. If one was licitly baptized and this baptism was recognized by the Church, one may receive the sacrament of Penance or Reconciliation before the Easter Vigil. There may also be combinations of these sacraments depending upon one's needs for entering the Church and depending upon what the bishop decides.

Getting back to Confession

This Sacrament of Penance, otherwise known as the Sacrament of Reconciliation is not simply entering into a physical confessional (a private space to speak to the priest regarding your past sins) and telling him what you did wrong. Moreover, one receives a typically mild penance to complete (most often prayers or a scripture reading to contemplate). At absolution (when the priest extends his hands and actually announces that your sins are forgiven) the person experiences a mystical blessing with graces (the actual sacrament). It is in this act that God forgives your sins and healing and reparation can begin.

This is a prominent and vital component to your purpose and cannot be overstressed. With sincere remorse "and a firm commitment to sin no more", you will encounter God's overwhelming love and forgiveness. For those who receive the sacrament of Penance with a contrite heart and religious disposition, reconciliation *"is usually followed by peace and serenity of conscience with strong spiritual consolation"* (Catechism of the Catholic Church, 1468). Jesus cares about you having peace and a clean soul. It is really what the Sacrament is about. It puts you in a repaired relationship status with God again. It is a "second chance" that one can frequently use in their lives. What a gift! St. Pope John Paul II recommended that people consider going to this Sacrament weekly or at least monthly. He himself went weekly. He knew the graces that come from it. You must be sincere and truly be sorry for your sins for this to be a valid sacrament.

If for some reason you are having difficulty in forgiving yourself regarding an unfortunate mistake, poorly thought-out action, something done pridefully, or just something spoken to someone you really wish you could take back, try praying the Litany of Forgiveness: "*Dear Lord Jesus Christ, I forgive myself, and I place myself at the foot of the holy cross, Lord please Bless me. Lord Jesus, I also forgive (so and so…), and I place he or she at the foot of the Holy Cross, please bless them as well".* This is a huge key for freedom, from pain and other issues. (Vicky Smith, 2024, O Crux Ave Media). It is not meant to be a substitute for confession. It serves however, to bridge the gap between times of sacrament attendance.

Let us consider the sin of poor St. Peter and how Jesus demonstrates his enduring love for him. I say poor St. Peter as his betrayal is the commonly pointed out example of disloyalty over the centuries. All through the generations people of faith have had to consider St. Peter's betrayal of our Lord. People then reflect on ways they too were unfaithful in some way to the Lord. In John 18: 25-27 we recall, "*Now Simon Peter was standing and warming himself. They asked him, 'You are not also one of his disciples, are you?' He denied it and said, 'I am not.' One of the slaves of the high priest, a relative of the man whose ear Peter had cut off, asked, 'Did I not see you in the garden with him?' Again, Peter denied it, and at that moment the cock crowed*". I can only imagine the self-loathing; the embarrassment, the bitterness St. Peter had to have experienced at that moment. He did not get to say, "*I am sorry*" to Jesus before He died on the cross.

This must have made St. Peter's remorse a hundred times worse to know that you just denied God and your best friend. But in reality, we are in the same shoes each time we do some sin that offends God. We are just as guilty. We often know in our heart that we are doing wrong. However, we are not strong enough to do the opposite. This is why we need to develop the virtues of strength and endurance.

Jesus's power is bigger than sin

In reflecting on our Lord's response and action to Peter, it comes after Jesus has risen from the dead. It comes in the form of merciful dialogue allowing Peter to express his sorrow and remorse. Jesus is so good and does not hold any resentment towards His friend. What an absolute remarkable Savior we have!

He already had asked Peter if he loved him two times before this and asks a third time. This really hammers it home to Peter. *"He said to him the third time, 'Simon son of John, do you love me?' Peter felt hurt because he said to him the third time, 'Do you love me?' and he said to him, 'Lord you know everything; you know that I love you.' Jesus said to him, 'Feed my sheep…'* (John 21: 17) We have to be able to forgive ourselves and truly believe Jesus has forgiven us. This gives us an example of endurance and love at the same time.

He forgives us and does not condemn us if we truly repent. It takes strength to forgive others as humans. It is a non-negotiable, however. Jesus expects us and demands that we forgive one another. No additional options. Purpose can come from these actions of compassion and humanity. A person displays perseverance in getting past betrayal and forgiving one another and is therefore Christ-like.

One might ask, how does Jesus instruct us to promote and develop these virtues? It is through faith and works. Jesus talks much about how having much faith can assist with having and holding these other virtues. When the apostles came to Jesus and asked Him why they could not cast out a certain demon, He states to them, "*Because of your little faith. For truly I tell you, if you have faith the size of a mustard seed, you will say to this mountain, 'Move from here to there', and it will move; and nothing will be impossible for you*" (Matthew, 17, 20-21). I could write another entire book on the subject of faith and works, but suffice it to say that one needs faith in God to exact and employ the strength, perseverance, and endurance that are being endorsed here. We will pick up the topic of faith, however, in a few chapters. We need to expound somewhat on this critical virtue.

Inexplicable supernatural perseverance

Let us especially consider for a moment the perseverance that our Lord possessed. It is something remarkable and extremely difficult to contemplate how our Lord was able to suppress one particular and disturbing thought. It is a supernatural aspect that this thought did not consume Him, or that He did not continually dwell on it. The thought being that He came to die for us and all that this dying and suffering entailed. Rather, He accepted that this was the Father's Will. He persevered like no one else could have.

I cannot imagine, that Jesus, knowing full well for thirty-three years that His main "job" or "duty" was to come to earth to be offered literally as a sacrifice of atonement for the human race's sin. Jesus lived for thirty-three years on earth before being crucified. This was God the Father's Will and Jesus completed it for the eternal benefit of humanity. This is why He is to be praised and honored forever!

Jesus was not dissuaded despite the incredulous ingratitude that the majority of humanity was showing at that time. Unfortunately, we also have shown this same ingratitude in our own current time. He was going to have to accomplish physical and mental endurance like no other in addition to the emotional suffering He was about to experience. The temptations that were piled upon Him during this same time we will never understand. The super unworthy actions and sinfulness of his followers and disciples both then and now in the future (including myself), were actions He could futuristically see.

Despite foreseeing our terrible deceitfulness in the Garden of Gethsemane (that is where He suffered out disloyalty and lukewarmness for every human created it is said), He went through and endured it all. He did not dodge a single torture or insult. Praise be to you Lord Jesus!

Can you imagine having the foreknowledge and the vivid reality that He was going to have to suffer death at the hands of professional Roman soldier executioners and torturers? If you did not already know it, the Romans's worst and most humiliating execution was death on a cross. Jesus knew this and chose it. He accepted this as the Father's Will for Himself and allowed it.

Recall if you will that Jesus knew He would be turned over to the Romans of the time because the Jews were not allowed to kill anyone as an occupied people. Can anyone fathom how our Lord could have continued to live out His ministry for the three years He lived and taught the apostles and disciples with this bit of knowledge always in the back of his mind? I cannot give the Lord enough thanks, honor, or glory for having persevered this much. Do you now see why Jesus demonstrated these virtues better than anyone else? He, without question, is the unsurpassed and most excellent example to follow.

Also recall that the apostles had witnessed many miracles and were really starting to believe that he might be the Messiah. Peter had recently stated that Jesus was the Christ. Yet they did not understand the idea of Jesus having to die for all our sins. *"From that time on, Jesus began to show his disciples that he must go to Jerusalem, and undergo great suffering at the hands of the elders and chief priests and scribes, and be killed, and on the third day be raised. And Peter took him aside and began to rebuke him, saying 'God forbid it, Lord! This must never happen to you'. But he turned and said to Peter, 'Get behind me, Satan!' you are a stumbling block to me; for you are setting your mind not on divine things but on human things'"* (Matthew 16, 21-24).

This is remarkable perseverance. Jesus continues on, and calms Himself down with Peter regarding Peter's human selfishness and not understanding the Messiah's true role. Remember that the Jewish people of the time thought that the coming of the Messiah meant their liberation from the Romans. They imagined the Messiah was going to reestablish a strong rank and file kingdom for themselves. Jesus's perseverance here provides us all an example of having to continue in certain situations where we know our own sacrifice is necessary amongst the circumstances. You can believe this added much undo stress for our Lord. He remarkably kept his overall composure and was able to continue onward.

It is in times of sheer perplexity where one needs to ask God for the grace and ability to continue the valiant fight. Jesus was educating the crowds, healing the sick, teaching His disciples, refuting the Jewish authorities and dodging the politicians at the time for their curiosity. He remarkably endured it all. You can find purpose in life knowing that Jesus Christ provides the exemplary model of accomplishing a remarkably difficult mission in the face of adversity and problematic people.

The good news is that while it is true that suffering and hardships can sometimes last a long time, Jesus will eventually provide relief and closure to situations. One can also find healing and become resilient with developing these virtues. It is said that the Lord never gives us more than we can handle. This is why we call on Him to assist us. We ask Him to get involved in our situations. This is why we are not to give up. We rather persist on finishing the good race as St. Paul states, *"As for me, I am already being poured out as a libation, and the time of my departure has come. I have fought the good fight, I have finished the race, I have kept the faith. From now on there is reserved for me the crown of righteousness, which the lord, the righteous judge, will give to me on that day, and not only to me but also to all who have longed for his appearing* (2 Timothy 6-8).

The mental aspect of endurance can often be the most punishing and taxing on our human limitations. In trying to deal with whatever is being required of us, the fatigue on our brains is overpowering. Sometimes these situations go on for months or years and it gets to the point where the relentless bombardments of stressful situations, or heartbreaking days can almost put us over the edge of the proverbial cliff. Nothing comes to mind more so than again thinking that our Lord had to deal with this thought of gathering these twelve apostles and trying to teach them over three years' time with disappointment after disappointment and then finding Himself entering Jerusalem the week before the customary Passover holiday.

How did Jesus not despair and break down on that Monday, or Tuesday, or Wednesday before Holy Thursday and Good Friday? Have you ever asked yourself how He endured this? How did He not lose His mind in worry and hopelessness? How did he keep his inner peace? Did He get any sleep at all that week? Or enough rest that He could function? It is like the man on death row who has come down to his final week on earth. How does he keep his panic from exploding or going insane about dying. We truly need to ask for the gift of serenity through our endurance. Jesus is our Divine example, our Prince of Peace, the Morningstar that breaks its light at the dawn. Thank you, Lord!

This yearning to do something to promote Jesus's attributes comes after years of falling down and asking for the strength to continue each and every day. I was in a place at one point in my life where I hoped God would intervene. I asked Him to take me home to heaven so I would not have to face the trials and impediments that each day brought. So many graces were provided to me through prayer and fasting (topics I will touch on later in the book). Enough grace so that I have continued on and have asked God to show me what He has left for me to accomplish for His Glory. Jesus's glory is the cross. If He still has a cross for me to bear, then I share in this glory.

I have come to believe that it is necessary to prove one's worthiness and gratitude back to God by fighting off evil each day. One has to draw on this Holy strength to fight this evil. I have come to understand that the value of our lives can be proven by accomplishing whatever comes to us each day.

Archbishop Fulton Sheen was a super star for Christ

Bishop Fulton Sheen (a most prominent Bishop in the 1950's as a television show host "*Life is worth living*") helps us critique purpose in our lives. His cause for Canonization is underway and will hopefully be named a Saint of the Church and dare I say maybe Doctor of the Church. Bishop Sheen had a famous quote regarding living with purpose, *"Let those souls who think their work has no value recognize that by fulfilling their insignificant tasks out of love of God, those tasks assume a supernatural worth. The aged who bear the taunts of the young, the sick crucified to their beds, the ignorant immigrant in the steel mill, the street cleaner and the garbage collector, the wardrobe mistress in the theater and the chorus girl who never had a line, the unemployed carpenter and the ash collector – all these will be enthroned above dictators, presidents, kings, and cardinals if a greater love of God inspires their humbler asks than inspires those who play nobler roles with less love"* (The Wisdom of Fulton Sheen, Matthew Kelly, pg. 43).

Divine Mercy's role in our purpose

I have learned from what the Lord himself describes as His greatest attribute, that of being a God of Mercy. In the diary of St. Sr. Faustina Kowalska, the Lord reveals that his greatest attribute is that of his Divine Mercy. "*Tell (all people), my daughter, that I am Love and Mercy itself. When a soul approaches Me with trust, I fill it with such an abundance of graces that it cannot contain them within itself, but radiates them to other souls.*" (Mercy My Mission, pg. 155).

I am a huge advocate to His Divine Mercy. In learning about this magnificent omnipotent mercy, I am inclined to point out the other divine qualities and virtues that demonstrate His love for His people. Namely, His virtues of strength, endurance, and perseverance. I have prayed frequently that the Holy Spirit might help me to make this topic fruitful and provide assistance to my besieged brothers and sisters. I pray not only that they overcome the evil that taunts them, but pray that the grace these holy virtues provide to joyfully and prosperously fulfill the purpose God has for each life that reads this writing.

Believe it or not, you have a special purpose in this life in his master plan! I have also asked our Blessed Mother, The Virgin Mary, The Mother of Jesus, to help me speak what will resonate with others for their sake. I have simply requested the graces be given to us through Her intercession to Her son on our behalf. She too is an example of a life that demonstrated the virtues of strength, perseverance, and endurance. Anyone who can watch Her son suffer and die and offer it all back to God without any fighting back deserves our attention as to the great virtues She possesses. I dedicate my life to Jesus through Her.

The way Jesus demonstrated how to live on earth shows us the way to put our head down and keep moving through the relentless storm. Truly considering all He went through and meditating on His actions and responses can give us some solid footing when we apply them to our own lives. Are you in a quandary in your lives where you believe even family and friends do not appreciate you? Do you feel attacked and unwanted? Time to turn to Jesus and ask Him to uphold you and give you strength. Time to ask Him to become involved in the situation and surrender all of your concerns to Him.

Contemplate if you will, what He had to endure when He began His ministry around His own hometown. It was here that family and friends knew Him and where He tried to teach and cure at Nazareth. They were not only rude and indifferent; they also refused to believe in Him. He told them He was God and they tried to kill Him. They utterly rejected His teachings and were offended at the idea that He might be the Messiah. Talk about a kick below the belt! *"They got up, drove him out of the town, and led him to the brow of the hill on which their town was built, so that they might hurl him off the cliff, but he passed through the midst of them and went on his way".* (Luke 4, 29-30).

Jesus demonstrates one of His first acts of perseverance after being shunned by family and friends in His hometown. The next time you are rejected by family and friends, ask the Lord to help the hurt and abandonment. Know that He experienced this before you as well. Ask for prayers that these same family and friends repair and restore the relationship with you. It is hard to forgive especially when attacked or despised by family. This might be your cross. Take time to pray for them even if it is difficult to do so.

Are there times in your life's vocation where you have or are having others wear you down? Are you being falsely accused? Are you being made a scapegoat or being blamed for things perhaps in the workplace, in a social circle, or in a family fight? Take courage in that Jesus again shows us His perseverance and endurance as He is misleadingly accused by the high priests of the time before his crucifixion.

If you recall, Jesus is arrested in the Garden of Gethsemane, on the Mount of Olives as described in the Gospel of Luke. Can you imagine being so scared and frightened that you are going to die a horrible death, and that most people will not even appreciate what you are going to accomplish for them? Imagine being so distraught and sorrowful that no one else knows what you are going through except God. You begin to sweat droplets of blood because of the anguish and torture you are experiencing. How can anyone not appreciate the strength that Jesus showed us in continuing on into the night that Holy Thursday? *"My Lord and My God!"* is all I can say when I think of His abandonment and desolation.

The mob of soldiers and Judas's cohort came and falsely accused Him on the spot. This scared the apostles so bad that first they went into defense mode for Jesus. Peter picked up a sword and cut the High Priest's servant's ear off, but then they all ran away after Jesus said to stop with the violence. The mob took Jesus to the high priest's house. Jesus was then denied by Peter three separate times. No one can say that Jesus never experienced betrayal. Jesus was then put into a dark dungeon all night awaiting His sentencing the next morning. For all of you who are experiencing violence, coercion, evil slandering, false accusations, and desertion by friends and family, I am here to remind you that Jesus endured all this even before his scourging. He suffered all this before the unthinkable walk to the cross where He was crucified. He knew all this was going to happen, and yet He continued to create His Church for three consecutive years before all this happened.

The point is that Jesus did all of this out of love for us. For those of you who are at the juncture where you are being rallied against by the evil of this time, call on Jesus to help you get through the trial and humiliations. Call on Him while being deserted by others. Know that your Savior went to His death having all these sorrows to suffer first. You might be in the same situation, but there is purpose in your suffering that we will discuss. There is a connection here to your purpose as there is a connection in Jesus's suffering. Jesus is demonstrating the way to get to your heavenly dwelling place.

Finally, let us consider what Jesus had to undergo after being held as a prisoner all night while awaiting His sentencing from the Roman Governor Pontious Pilate. When one reads about hostages being taken and the terror they face in the midst of some political or private power manipulation, it is usually the case that people are simply pawns in the evil that is being bargained. These people suffer as innocent bystanders. There is usually little value put on their lives in the big picture for those holding hostages captive. So was the case for our Lord Jesus. While He was completely innocent, the Jews felt that having one person die for their cause (the cause that meant the Romans would continue to quell and suppress the Jews and keep them morally beat down) was better for them as a whole than having many people die from an uprising. This was their excuse. They even bargained to trade out Jesus for a murderer and guerilla type war criminal named Barabas. Yes, there was a political aspect to Jesus's death as well.

So, Jesus gets swapped out for Barabas in the middle of Pontius Pilate's interrogation. This interrogation is one in which Jesus portrays for us his super endurance and strength. Picture the scene where Jesus has been suffering in the Garden until about midnight. From there He goes and is first questioned at the high priest's home not to mention being beaten there by a few guards. He is then betrayed by one of His best friends three different times, and abandoned by the apostles. He is put in a dank and dark prison cell until morning when Pontius Pilate grills Him.

From there the Governor's scrutiny takes place where Pilate is trying to figure out who Jesus is. Jesus, however, does not divulge much information as it is fairly apparent the uselessness of trying to explain things. "*Pilate asked him, 'So you are a king?' Jesus answered , 'You say that I am a king. For this I was born, and for this I came into the world, to testify to the truth. Everyone who belongs to the truth listens to my voice.; Pilate asked him, 'What is truth?'* (John 18: 37-38) Jesus has consented to His death sentence and is ready to walk the dolorosa (small road to the area where He will be crucified), but not before Pilate has Him flogged and where soldiers put the crown of thorns on His head.

It is here where Roman soldiers torment and beat Him to a bloody unrecognizable being at a scourging pillar. I think the Passion by Mel Gibson is not far from reality according to some mystics who were able to see Jesus's scourging at the pillar. He receives a crown of thorns to mock His Kingship over the Jews. Some mystics describe this crown as hawthorn thorns and marine planks that are about an inch or longer in length. While its woven and formed it is beat down on His head to the point where the thorns pierce the flesh and skull bone. After being almost beaten to death, Jesus still has to carry on. Jesus gives us a new definition for the word strength.

Jesus shows us incredible endurance and perseverance

He meets His mother and other women friends who are trying to bring Him some relief in His agony. To think of all He has endured in just the last twelve hours is incomprehensible and beyond one's understanding of what one person could physically, emotionally, and mentally endure. However, He is not done persevering yet.

From having to carry the weight of the cross, which was probably well over one hundred pounds (or at least the part Jesus was forced to support and lug uphill was this heavy), He fell at least three times. He had to continue on. St. Bernard of Clairvaux (1090 -1153 AD, Catholicculture.org), (a mystic to whom Jesus gave special graces to know things about

Jesus's sufferings at His Passion), discloses that Jesus revealed to him that He has a special wound on his left shoulder. *"I had on My Shoulder, while I bore My Cross on the Way of Sorrows, a grievous Wound, which was more painful that the others, and which is not recorded by men".* (Pieta Prayer Booklet, St. Bernard of Clairvaux). Can you imagine having to carry a large piece of raw and unfinished lumber on an open wound that most likely was opened to the bone? Thank you, Jesus for your example of sheer fortitude in strength! But it was far from being over....

Here is where it borders on getting "outside" one's perception of what one person could endure. Jesus, once the Roman soldiers get Him to the spot where He is to be crucified, is then forcefully held down. Having His wrists tied off, He is stretched left and right where He submits to being held down while two or three soldiers nail his hands off with large spikes. Can you imagine large railroad spike type nails piercing your bone and muscles?

The soldiers most likely tie off His wrists to support the body weight on the cross. Can you imagine the natural urge, the instinctive wanting to pull away from this pain as you felt and heard this happening to your own body? Then to further imagine this also happening to your feet and legs. I cannot imagine my feet bones separating and the pressure put on the tissue. I can barely write this as I think of the excruciating torture methods used on our Lord as He did not fight back, but offered it all up to the Father. This in reparation for our sinfulness. I love you Lord for what you have done for all of us. I am truly sorry for doing all of this to you! How can I make it up to you?

Finally, after hanging on a tree and enduring at least three hours of pain and heartbreaking distress, (The Gospel of St. Mark tells us that Jesus was crucified at 9 a.m. and did not pass away until 3 p.m. making it a possibility that Jesus suffered for six hours on the cross) Jesus gives up His Life. Other Gospels state that Jesus was hung on the Cross at 12 p.m., but there is discrepancy on which hours each Gospel uses to account when Jesus was first nailed to the cross. Jesus tells some mystics that He suffered on the cross for three hours. Either way, our Lord heroically endured pain and anguish beyond comprehension for a long time. Someday we will ask Him and know for sure and honor His Holy wounds in person.

After putting up with the scoffing and mockery of the Jewish passer-byes and the soldiers, after first being derided and reviled by both criminals executed with Him, He then forgives one of the criminals. This thief is known in tradition as the "good thief", or Dismas. Our Lord is so compassionate even in immense pain and distress. Dismas has a change of heart and asks Jesus to remember him when enters His kingdom. Jesus replies to Dismas, *"Truly I tell you, today you will be with me in Paradise" (Luke 23 43).* Remarkable mercy from our Lord is shown and it is recorded in history.

Finally, Jesus gives His Blessed Mother to St. John (a symbol to us all that we have the Queen of Heaven as our spiritual mother). In other-words, in so giving His mother to St. John the apostle, it represents that Jesus gives us, His brothers and sisters, His mother. This gesture is indeed a request for us to take to heart what our heavenly Mother asks of us and to see to it that She is revered, honored, and obeyed. She needs us to help Her fight evil and make Her son known. Jesus has designated His mother to crush the head of the serpent. She will go on in history to continue to draw Her sons and daughters back to God.

Jesus commends His Spirit over to the Father. Jesus, is the ultimate and epitome of super perseverance, endurance, and strength. Lord, I cannot nor will I ever be able to, tell you how grateful I am that you did this for me and my human family! "*When it was noon, darkness came over the whole land until three in the afternoon. At three o'clock Jesus cried out with a loud voice, 'Eloi, Eloi, lema sabachthani?'.... Then Jesus gave a loud cry and breathed his last*" (John 1533-34, 37).

The hope is that in rewriting these accounts of our Lord's passion, it will help others come to an encouraging conclusion. The hope is that whatever they may be facing in life, that they will consider all that the Lord did for the salvation of their soul. This alone should provide purpose for them to continue.

While things can be long enduring and while some of what people go through can take months and years to get through, we can know that Jesus persevered first and foremost and achieved His end for our ultimate right to get to heaven. This should give you consolation above all other things! Secondly, we can call out to Him, day and night and we must. We are to ask Him to intervene, and remedy the situation with our own prayers, fasting, and sacrifice added to the process. This solution will alleviate anything that threatens us. Praise be to you Jesus Christ. For by the means of your sufferings and strength, we have the example and ability to get to heaven and even achieve a high place in eternity by following your Holy virtues. Thank you for being so strong for us!

God Our Father

In closing this chapter, I am also inclined to write regarding God the Father's providence. I would argue that God the Father suffered with Jesus and helped Him provide for us all these virtues. He is our loving Creator who is ultimately so very patient and truly slow to anger despite our extremely sinful ways and actions. He created us to have a loving relationship with Him for all eternity, and has given us various graces and means, (mainly through Jesus) that help us defeat the enemy. I am extremely excited to meet God the Father, and terrified as well. I am embarrassed of my past sins knowing that He created me, but at the same time look to Him as a dad who is proud of us for whatever reason. If nothing else, that we fought evil until the end of our lives, and chose God to be with in the end. Father Mark -Mary Ames, CFR. in his great book *The Father*, says this about God our Father: *"The beauty of the Catholic Faith revealed in the Word of God and the teachings of the Church, is that it does not simply give us a set of guidelines for self-fulfillment. Rather, Jesus comes to give us the fullness of truth that we have a heavenly Father who loves us and is the best of fathers. The Church's teachings and her guidance give us the path to enter into and remain in this relationship with God, our Father, receiving the fullness of his grace as we journey through this life toward our eternal home"* (pg. 2). Thank you, God the Father for our lives and the lives of our family members, and for the lives of our good and faithful friends!

The Holy Spirit, The Paraclete

Finally, the Holy Spirit fills us with His love and who prompts us never to give up our daily struggle. It is the Holy Spirit and our Guardian angels directed by God who point out ways to overcome the Father of lies, the one in whom we constantly battle in the fight for our soul. Therefore, go each day joyfully demonstrating these three virtues to solidify your relationship with the Lord. In so doing, your life will provide an example to others to continue to be a champion for the Lord who created you. "*And he said to them, 'Go into all the world and proclaim the good news to the whole creation. The one who believes and is baptized will be saved; but the one who does not believe will be condemned*" (Mark 16: 15-16). It is this Spirit who is God Himself and is the third person of the Holy Trinity, Jesus's and the Father's Spirit. And as mysterious and incomprehensible as this may seem, He wants to give us the grace and gifts that spiritually bring us to a supernatural level! He is also known as the Paraclete, the Spirit of Truth. Please recall that this reading is based on truth and that the truth will ultimately bring you to fulfillment. Jesus said, "*When the Paraclete comes, the Spirit of truth who comes from the Father-and whom I Myself will send from My Father-He will bear witness on my behalf...He will guide you to all truth*" (John 15, 26-27; 16: 13)

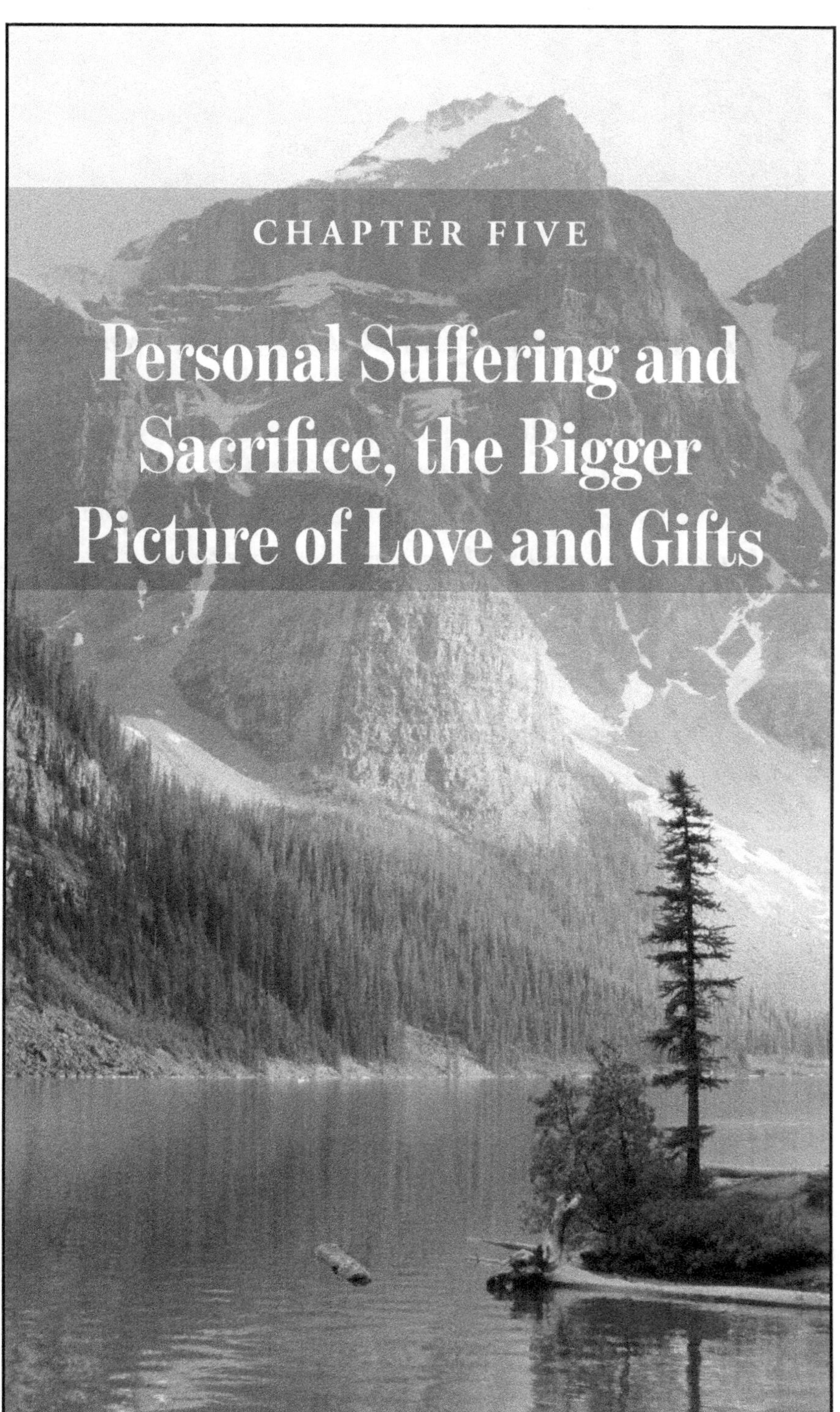

CHAPTER FIVE

Personal Suffering and Sacrifice, the Bigger Picture of Love and Gifts

Form your conscience with offering suffering and sacrifice to God and truth will become apparent

Maybe one of the most common or popular questions we hear asked of all time: *Why is their suffering in this life?* Or maybe: *Why, if there is a good, gracious, and all-powerful loving God, does He allow suffering? Or perhaps, why do we have to sacrifice so much to get ahead in this life?* Weeks and months can be spent trying to probe and examine this philosophic topic. However, like many facts already covered in this book, let us "cut to the chase" on these subjects.

Again, I need to reiterate that it is essential that the reader hear out this information before judging the content. It is true that some of this matter is the exact opposite of what you will hear others say. That is why it is important to take it to your conscience. The devil wants you to feel awkward or antiquated or just plain weird with some of these concepts. It is not easy to digest something that sounds foreign or counter-cultural, but that is exactly why you need to weigh these subjects in your heart. You will understand that what is spoken is truth. Ask your guardian angel to help you know. Quiet your mind and soul and ask Jesus who is truth to enlighten you regarding each situation and issue.

To take what is presented regarding true suffering and sacrifice, and to let these two concepts infuse into our souls, our inner beings through meditation and prayer is what will reveal their authenticity. It is in considering the significance of these two realities, heaven versus hell, that one very much needs to be enlightened and edified by the truth. We live in times of extreme confusion, times of extraordinary phenomenon that are occurring, and one needs to latch on to the only true rock that will be there when the waves stop crashing on the shore. That rock is Jesus Christ and He will be that solid and edified truth.

Let us look at the worldly definitions for two experiences that are part of our human condition. The definition of suffering according to the Oxford Languages Dictionary—*Suffering as a noun* = the state of undergoing pain, distress or hardship, *as a verb* = an experience or to be subjected to something bad or unpleasant or to tolerate. Then we review the term sacrifice. *Sacrifice as a noun* = an act of slaughtering an animal or person, or surrendering a possession, *as a verb* = an act of giving up something valued for the sake of something else regarded as more important or worthy. These are the worldly definitions that paint a picture that only negativity comes from these two actions. Both have bad connotations in the worldly viewpoint. What we need to illustrate is that there are positive results from these when applied in a manner and frame of mind that one chooses when undergoing these certainties. Jesus obtained for us forgiveness of our sins and acquired our ability to enter heaven based on suffering and sacrifice. He used the virtues we are discussing to perfect these both. Both are very meritorious and noble, and in the spiritual realm, are the actions that gain us our crown and honors in Heaven. Did you know that the angels wish they could suffer and sacrifice? They are spiritual beings and cannot participate in these types of actions that we both flesh and spiritual beings can accomplish. Try and ponder that thought!

Suffering done well has much merit

We as created beings need to come to the conclusion that suffering exists (we will get to sacrifice as well), and that it is unavoidable to certain extents. While we can dodge and avoid it, there are times that in envelopes us without our full consent. To get to this matter rather quickly, one needs to consider our first parents. The actions of Adam and Eve. You as the reader need to know that our God does not waste our time or our lives. That is, suffering has meaning and is not a fruitless punishment. Although some of the punishment for our sins is having to suffer from ultimately disobeying God, we can otherwise put the suffering that we encounter to commendable use. We are, however, fairly good at wasting time and energy ourselves, but not God. This is why one needs to recognize the value that suffering can generate.

The truth of the matter is that Adam and Eve were our first parents, and we find ourselves descendants in one way, shape or form from these individuals. Scientists still debate the genetic divergence of humans. More DNA studies and findings are consistent with biblical history, however. Recent studies of single nucleotide polymorphisms (SNPs) are believed to be representative of the total human DNA genome. These studies and others have shown that the difference in DNA between any two humans is amazingly low (only about .1%) and this is proportionately low considering many other species from fruit flies to chimpanzees. (Dr. Elizabeth Mitchell, *Did We All Come from Adam and Eve*, 2013). Unfortunately, we have a disposition to follow our first parents. Thus, we follow sin as well because we are not always obedient to God's laws and commands. These laws and commandments are for our own good to keep us from evil.

In Genesis, (the first book of the Bible) Adam and Eve ultimately disobeyed God's one request not to eat of a particular tree in the middle of paradise. They had everything else at their disposal. However, human selfishness and a form of greed took over.

All Adam and Eve had to do was trust in God. He had already told both to stay away from the one tree in the middle of the garden. He was testing them for their loyalty and love. He forbade them to eat from and touch one single tree "*...the tree of the knowledge of good and* *evil, you shall not eat".* (Genesis, 2:17). The one tree they were supposed to stay away from became a deadly curiosity when they decided not to listen to God, but rather the devil. In all fairness, they were deceived by the ultimate deception that they could be like God Himself. They did however choose to disobey.

Our first parents fell prey to Satan the devil. Why does Satan have our number and want us to disobey God? It is because he cannot and will not recover from his own disobedience to God. He wants us all to suffer eternally. That is why we must resist with all our fiber. While we cannot blame our parents for human weakness, this ultimately caused the human race to take on suffering from that moment forward because they sinned against God in defying His commands.

Sin is lawlessness, and we need God's law. It is that simple

Sin equals separation from God and separation from God equals suffering. This is why we strive not to sin, because we offend the one who loves us unconditionally, the one we should love with our whole heart, mind, and soul. The truth is, the devil is still trying to get us to separate ourselves from God. Those of us who have sensed this separation and realize the eternal consequences do not approve of it one bit! This is why we sometimes suffer and sacrifice, but with the help of our virtues, we actually become grace-filled and are more focused on loving God all the more and avoiding the "near occasions of sin".

Keep in mind that this original sin would have kept us all out of Heaven. In spite of this, God rescued us from being eternally miserable and in complete loss. Please recall that because of original sin, we have a debt that, until paid, would prevent us from acquiring heaven if we are not baptized. The Good News (I should say the news that should make one ecstatically joyful) is that Jesus Christ was sent to us and suffered death first. The amazing part is that He defeated death, because He rose again from the dead with the power of God the Father! The idea that God sent His son as the Messiah to save us is another unique concept that shows how much He cares for the human race. Would you send your only kid to save a bunch of ungrateful strangers knowing that he would be ridiculed and eventually killed after being tortured just for telling people the truth?

Gratitude to God...a sure sign you are on the right path

We have to dive deeper into our souls and ask the Holy Spirit to uncover how much God loves us. Not to diverge from this concept, St. Francis De Sales puts this whole concept into focus when, in his book *The Introduction to the Devote Life,* he states how much we need to be grateful to our heavenly Father. In the first of many meditations, this one being about our creation, he alludes to showing this gratitude. *"Consideration – 1. Consider that a certain number of years ago you were not yet in the world and that your present being was truly nothing. My soul, where were we at that time? The world had already existed for a long time, but of us there was as yet nothing. 2. God has drawn you out of that nothingness to make you what you now are and he has done so solely out of his own goodness and without need of you. 3. Consider the nature God has given to you. It is the highest in this visible world; it is capable of eternal life and of being perfectly united to his Divine Majesty."*

Then after the meditation, St. Francis has the person act on the consideration for the meditations. *"Affections and Resolutions – 1. Humble yourself profoundly before God, and like the Psalmist say with all your heart: 'Lord, before you I am truly nothing. How were you mindful of me so as to create me? Alas, my soul, you were engulfed in the ancient nothing and you would still be there if God had not drawn you out of it. What could you have done in that nothingness? 2. Return thanks to God. My great and good Creator, how great is my debt to you since you were moved to draw me out of nothing and by your mercy to make me what I am! What can I ever do to bless your holy name in a worthy manner and to render thanks to your immense mercy?'"* (Pg. 53) The point is to be mindful that you were nothing until God created you, and you give back to Him as much as you can in thanksgiving. This is where suffering and sacrifice make the most sense, and reciprocating is done because of this love for God.

Baptism first

In coming full circle on the concept of suffering, Jesus bravely withstood His suffering and highly demonstrated those three virtues we discussed in Chapter Two. He came and was baptized with water by His cousin St. John the Baptist. This was done so that anyone who believes in Him and is likewise baptized in the name of the Father and the Son and the Holy Spirit, can become one of his brothers/ sisters adopted by the Heavenly Father. We acknowledge this adoption and pray for it. As a matter of fact, at the Catholic celebration of the mass we implore God for it. In the Eucharistic prayer during the mass, the priest invokes God the Father when he asks on our behalf that God "make us co-heirs to eternal life". We discussed this concept previously, but let us try and unpack this baptism stuff with a little more insight.

Jesus tries to tell a high-ranking leader of the Jews, a Pharisee named Nicodemus who has taken a liking to Jesus about being baptized. Nicodemus is curious in Jesus and is convinced that He is from God. This is worth noting because Nicodemus is not like the other Pharisees. He is not necessarily worried or threatened, but wants to know more about our Lord. He starts to ask Jesus some questions. Jesus somewhat cuts him off and leap frogs his questions by telling Nicodemus that he needs to be "*born from above*" before he can enter the kingdom of God (John 3 : 3). Jesus alludes to the need of being baptized into God's family because of Jesus's new Church.

We established that Baptism is a sacrament. The sacraments give us sanctifying grace. Sanctifying grace means a spiritual grace that helps one become holy so we can eventually live with God. Certain sacraments leave a spiritual mark on our soul that lasts forever. The mark on our soul at Baptism is like a permanent stamp that identifies us as belonging to Christ (Baltimore Catechism, pgs. 113-114).

Belonging to Christ is the gist of our purpose and if we belong to Him, He takes us to the Father's House where we are told there are many dwelling places. Enough for all of us! *Jesus answered, "Very truly I tell you, no one can enter the Kingdom of God without being born of water and Spirit. What is born of the flesh is flesh, and what is born of the Spirit is spirit. Do not be astonished that I said to you, 'You must be born from above'" (John 3: 5-7).* This whole idea is still a mystery, and we do not understand it fully, and anyone who says they understand it completely is lying. However, Jesus comes out and says it point blank..."*Do not be astonished*". In other words, He is saying, *"Just have faith in what I am telling you, and you will eventually be rewarded for trusting and following me."* Baptism sets us apart from non-believers. Baptism allows us to be forgiven from our original sin from Adam and Eve.

Original sin is something we forget about

Again, we need to exceedingly realize that we have a heavenly Father who loves us! Did you however, ever contemplate that you were ransomed by suffering and sacrifice? Original sin is complicated. And somehow this original sin is passed down through the generations. Baptism, however, breaks this sin's grasp on our soul. Our first parents were deceived enough to go against what God commanded. They certainly did not think through the ramifications of disobedience. Jesus was obedient unto death. Another virtue that our Lord exemplifies through and through. So, do not act rebellious. Demonstrate humility.

Stand down when tempted. Do not act. Be strong and persevere past that which is selfish evil.

Let us discuss some this redeeming act of Jesus and the ransom that He provided. He substituted obedience for disobedience and embraced the Father's plan in salvation by dying for our sins. While the ransom was paid by Jesus, we still have to try make ourselves worthy to be saved even in our unworthiness as humans. In other words, while Jesus completed this redemptive action for us by His death on the cross, we need to try to prove ourselves worthy of this ransom act with the choices we make. We try and become worthy of Him paying off our debt.

Cannot earn salvation, but can strive to become worthy of the gift of redemption and be saved by God

I know some Protestants and even Catholics are going to go crazy reading this with the thought that you have to "earn" salvation, or "earn" your heaven, but there is a difference between this and striving to do God's will. Earning salvation is not what is being suggested here. I am not stating that you can earn your salvation, because it is ultimately God who chooses those to be saved. While we cannot earn our own salvation, we still are making a choice to choose God. We also choose to ask for forgiveness and demonstrate our allegiance to God vs. the evil one.

We choose to do good deeds, avoid known sinfulness, and demonstrate faith in choosing God. It is the opposite of the concept that some errantly retain that suggests that, "*once I believe and choose God, then I am saved no matter what other poor choices I make in life*". We show that we are serious about our worthiness to accept Jesus's act for us by never stopping to ask for His forgiveness until our dying day. We demonstrate we are serious about our attempting to become worthy in the sense of making choices for God and not for our own selfishness. We continue to improve and do good, trying to please God and listen to His commands. We choose God and attempt to become worthy, signifying our allegiance and love, and ultimately doing His will versus going against His Will. Jesus is worthy, and we strive to become like Him.

We reveal our true selves and our intent by having faith and eventually asking forgiveness in the Sacrament of Penance. First, we may have had the sacrament of Baptism by the decision of our parents or guardians. These are acts of faith, and by demonstrating this faith we have a justification for being a *"friend of God"*, (James, 2:23). But we also need to have works in our life and both faith and works are required to demonstrate that you are worthy of this ransom. St. James tells us that we need to have faith and works to demonstrate our worthiness. *"You see that a person is justified by works and not by faith alone"* (James 2:24).

Where am I going with this? It is this. You have to believe in the name of Jesus, because He ransomed you. No one else did. You must also do the Will of His Father in order to be judged worthy of entering the heavenly kingdom and saying "yes" to the ransom that Jesus provided for you.

Besides being created out of the love of God, both your faith in God and the works you do ultimately for Him are what make you worthy of life eternal. Sometimes suffering and sacrifice are needed on our part to do the Will of the Father. Be warned that even believing in Jesus and this ransom will cost you in earthly terms. It is, however, part of acknowledging that you belong to the team that wins! *"Not everyone who says to me, 'Lord, Lord', will enter the kingdom of heaven, but only the one who does the will of my Father in heaven" (Matthew 7: 21).* It is God's will that your obedience and allegiance to Him are reflected in your faith in Him. The works you carry out prove that you love Him and want to give back to Him for all blessings received. Pray that you might know what works He wants you to complete for Him!

Now let us get back to suffering and sacrifice. God did not want the destruction of His created children. He sent His only Begotten Son Jesus Christ to spare us this eternal catastrophe. Jesus was always part of the Holy Trinity, yet God His Father sent Him to ultimately suffer and make that sacrifice we desperately needed. Truly a mystery, but it comes with believing in Him.

To go a little more in depth on these conclusions, let us consider the following to supplement the illustration. Original sin injured the world and society so much that things such as toil and labor and conflict now became part of our daily lives. Nothing blissful comes with the results of losing paradise. I know, deep down, no one is satisfied with this outcome of temporarily losing paradise except the devil. It is still a mystery that all this came about. We lack the details of all activities in Paradise at that time. We know however, that the devil was thrown out of heaven down to earth and therefore, he was around to muster some sort of revenge on God by deceiving us. He wants to take from God anything he can.

Sin is not justifiable, so seek to overcome your continued sinful habits

Someday I hope to look St. Adam in the eye and ask him what was really the driving factor in eating the fruit? Were you trying to please your wife? Did you really think that you would be like God? Were you just being rebellious and acting out against a rule? Didn't you believe God was going to say something? Was the devil in the serpent that convincing? Apparently so. The point is, there are many reasons why we sin, and none of them are justifiable. We offend God when we should be looking to please Him.

It is neither here nor there at this point, because we are all subject to the effects of this one original sin. I do not blame our original parents, because they were betrayed by the evil one, who himself disobeyed God and lost the privileges of Heaven for eternity. He knowingly confronted God and tried to make himself above God.

He, the evil one, along with one-third of the angels were thrown out of heaven, because they made the choice to go against God. They, however, did not get a second chance to redeem themselves. Do you know why? It is because angels had full knowledge already after being created that God was the Supreme and Ultimate Being. They, however, still decided to side with Lucifer and try and obtain more power and glory. We alluded to this concept earlier in the writing. This is why these disobeying angels can no longer be called angels, but rather demons. Fortunately for our sake Jesus became the "new" Adam, and His mother the "new" Eve who demonstrate for us complete obedience towards God. Thank you again Lord Jesus for your faithfulness. Please give me the grace to sin no more!

Thank God for second chances

We humans at least have a second chance to ask forgiveness based on the ransom we have in Jesus. It is all true, *"And war broke out in heaven: Michael and his angels fought against the dragon. The dragon and his angels fought back, but they were defeated and there was no longer any place for them in heaven. That great dragon was thrown down, that ancient serpent, who is called the Devil and Satan, the deceiver of the whole world – he was thrown down to earth, and his angels were thrown down with him" (Revelations 12, 7-9).* It was inevitable then at that point that some human was going to break the commandments of God and therefore we cannot blame Adam and Eve. I am strictly speaking about odds here. The Devil was cunning and relentless in his pursuit to bring down the human race, but no one is greater than our God. He had a plan, and the plan brings us back to Him in the end.

These sinful consequences, however, result in the human race having to suffer all kinds of things. Sorrow and sadness, aches and pains, symptoms of illness and disease, betrayal and deception, abandonment and loneliness, hot and cold, and so on. Sometimes suffering can be so overwhelming, that it can overtake us and we succumb to the intensity.

More to understand regarding suffering and sacrifice

The remarkable and truthful good news is that suffering is valued and can give one a great deal of purpose in one's life. When we "*offer up*" our sufferings and sacrifices and "*unite*" these to God, we can ask that these be "*applied*" to help others who might be suffering more than we are. When we make an effort to consciously tell God He can freely use these sufferings and sacrifices, we "*give*" to Him an offering. He then does marvelous deeds and works on account of this spiritual generosity.

We give a great gift back to Him for the sake of atoning for our sins or the sins of our brothers and sisters. Without going into this now, we can offer our sufferings and sacrifices for those who are dying that they might have special help and graces at their particular judgement. Or, we can offer up these sufferings and sacrifices for the souls that are in the state of purgation. We would say these souls are in neither heaven at the moment nor hell, but in Purgatory. This is another more in-depth topic that will require the reader to do some additional research, but this state is an awesome mercy of God.

Make no mistake, the sins in the world compound the evil that is wrought. God, however, can make good come from these offerings when one is willing to "*give these*" sufferings and sacrifices back to the Lord as a sort of gift. The true gift becomes ours, however, as we will explore some more.

When you are willing to provide these aches, pains, and hurts back to God, He "*converts*" them in a most special way. We will not understand the good that comes from these offerings until we see how God utilized them for others. It is like the best *"extra credit"* we could ever get. Suffering and sacrifice have so much value that the good angels wish they had the opportunity to participate in such a notion. Jesus reveals this to St. Sr. Faustina in her diary, *"Daughter, I need sacrifice lovingly accomplished because that alone has meaning for Me. Enormous indeed are the debts of the world which are due to Me; pure souls can pay them by their sacrifice, exercising mercy in spirit"* (Mercy My Mission, pg. 176).

Consider this. Suffering does not always equal tears and or pain. It can also be accounted for in perhaps abstaining from something you really enjoy (a sacrifice if you will) and that abstinence is applied to another person's wellbeing. Or, perhaps fasting from some food for the sake of helping one to see their own error and sinful ways. Or putting up and bearing with something that is a super pet peeve. How about tolerating someone's annoying habits? All take on the aspect of a sacrifice.

Combining suffering and sacrifice with the virtues of strength, perseverance, and endurance

Maybe it is going out of your way to visit someone because you know they could really use someone to talk to or be with at the moment. It could be as great as anonymously donating some huge amount of money, or as meek as reading a story to a bedridden child. Do any of these actions remind you of the virtues we are discussing in this book? Persevering, enduring, and having the strength to undergo these experiences. These actions produce good, and that is one of the keys we need to get to the dwelling place. These actions and others can also be called corporal (meaning of the flesh) and spiritual acts of mercy. (There is actually a list of these mercies that the Catholic Church encourages one to endeavor in, as they reflect things that Christ would do, or ask us to do).

It is not a coincidence that these virtues can help provide a positive outcome if you consciously apply your suffering and sacrifices for the wellbeing of someone. The great Archbishop, now Venerable, Fulton Sheen stated this regarding our actions and thought processes, "*We begin to act differently when we recognize the immensity of our possibilities*" (Kelly, August 6th, pg. 75). When we accumulate these good actions and we *"have our hands full"* of good works these help atone for our own sinfulness. We want to be able to reflect back upon these actions when we undergo our judgement with God one day. We already discussed that we do not believe that we can *"earn"* our salvation. However, our faith and good works can demonstrate to God that we believed in Him and wanted to do His will to please Him. Albeit, we still need to be free of serious (mortal) sin before we take our last breath.

This concept of sin being mortal and less than mortal (venial) is another topic that requires some study and further inquiry. To be without mortal sin is imperative to eternal life with God. It is not within the scope of these pages to speak in-depth on the issue, however, one is required to keep one's soul clean and innocent. This is a state of spiritual cooperativeness that will allow the Holy Spirit to help you understand more right from wrong. The smaller venial sins, while still sin, can be alleviated by not only confession, but by the taking of the Holy Eucharist.

Keep an open mind regarding avoiding sinful things and keep from offending God the best you can. Try reading the Ten commandments again, because they are absolutely still relevant and applicable! They are from God! Remember this, "G*race is something given as a gift from God that helps us, but sinning is something that is stolen from God and something that offends Him*". (Father Richard Simon, from the *Father Simon Says Show*, Relevant Radio).

Important distinctions to make regarding certain sufferings and sacrifices

Finally, the author here recognizes that in life there are times when suffering and sacrifice are not always wholesome in the context that sometimes there is an unnatural or non-appropriate cause for the suffering and sacrifice. I would be remiss not to acknowledge that sometimes very troubling and absolutely evil things can happen to people that cause them to suffer and have to sacrifice. By no means does this author suggest that these need to be tolerated. Things such as verbal, physical or sexual abuse are not to be excused. People do not have to endure these types of hostilities. Awful and unspeakable acts such as rape, sexual slavery, and or child abuse and other reprehensible acts are not what are being asked to be tolerated or sacrificed back to God. God does not will these types of sinful acts.

While there are people who have undergone these types of travesties and do offer up their suffering, these are not in any way suggested by the author that one should have to live with or allow these things to happen to them. This is another realm of suffering and sacrifice that has its origin in evil. We will do well if we can prevent any and all of these types of sins. This has to be made perfectly clear that if these are something you have experienced or are experiencing, then the proper authorities need to be notified. It is critical to have them assist in ending this type of suffering.

This type of suffering is not something that needs to be sacrificial. Love for one's neighbor includes helping that person be removed from any and all types of criminal acts of violence, hurt and hate. This includes not forcing one to have an abortion and snuffing out a life. There are no reasons known to have an abortion. It is my duty as an author to help you understand this. Abortion is actually an intrinsic evil.

An intrinsic evil is one that cannot be justified. If you have happened to have had an abortion, there is forgiveness with Jesus through the Sacrament of Penance that we have discussed already. There are also programs available to help heal spiritually and mentally, even if it was years ago that the abortion happened. Rachel's Vineyard is one of those programs. One can research the nearest opportunity to attend one of these events. Do yourself a huge favor and seek these healing ministries. They are created to help with that burden you carry every day, and may not realize it. Praise be to Jesus for His magnificent mercy!

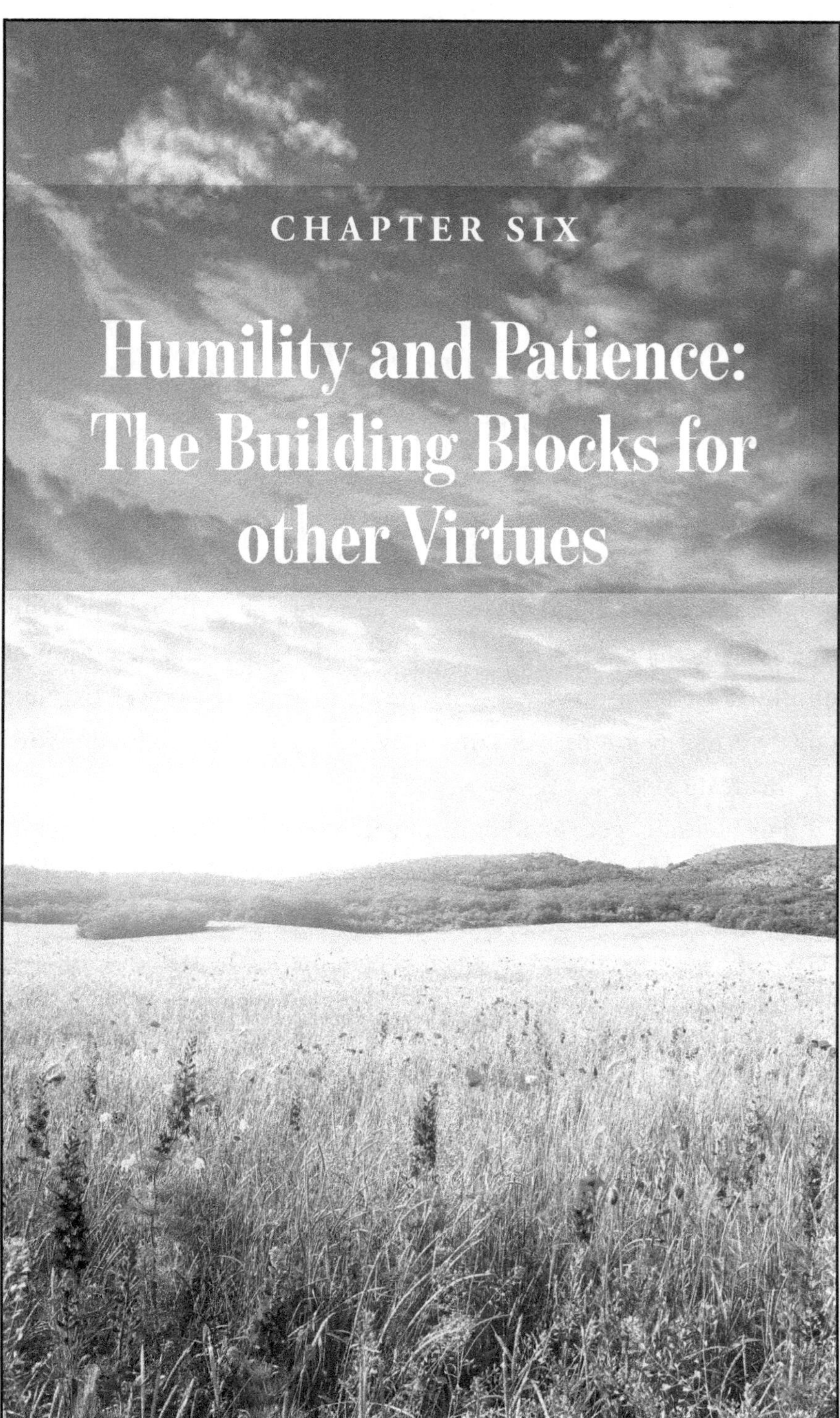

CHAPTER SIX

Humility and Patience: The Building Blocks for other Virtues

God loves humility

Have you ever considered that God knows all things, is all independent and formidable, and needs none of us. He is invincible and is infinite in His omnipotence. He is sovereign. He does not need us, but we need Him. Despite His great sovereignty, He never forces us to love Him or choose Him? Our God is supremely humble. How can a God that created all things give His creatures this freedom to choose Him or not? It is because God is the definition of humility. He is all-powerful and yet, He gives us the power to make our own life decisions. Amazing may not be a strong enough word for this reality.

His Humility goes hand in hand with His patience for us. He gives us chance after chance to want to live a good and holy life, to say "No" to the enemy and all the false promises that are presented to us. He is so patient with us, that even when we are the furthest from Him and are doing the complete opposite of what He has shown us, He still calls out to us to turn around. We are truly prodigal and often squander goodness and grace that He wants to shed on us. He calls out to us all the way to our final breath for us to love Him back. This is supernatural patience and our God displays this when it comes His creatures.

This, however, does not mean He will not correct us or punish us if we push His Justice. The great news is that His Mercy has long endurance. Scripture tells us that He is slow to anger. Many of us keep trouncing His offer of mercy and change as if we have no reason to care about our final destination. We need to turn the boat around before it goes over the proverbial falls and end up smashed at the bottom. The point is that we need humility to see our faults, failures and sinfulness. We need humility to ask for forgiveness. We need this forgiveness to get to heaven. *"Humility is truth, or seeing ourselves as we really are-not as we think we are, nor as the public believe us to be, or as our press notices us" (*Archbishop Fulton Sheen, Kelly, pg. 57).

The need to become patient individuals

We need the patience to continue to be humble. We need patience to continue to work hard at doing good and avoiding evil. We need to again emulate Jesus with these virtues to make the other previously discussed virtues work. It takes time to refine these two particular virtues. Then again, people are born with various levels of these virtues. One's demeanor is influenced by one's environment, and yet each of these virtues can be given as gifts by God in different amounts. Jesus again shows us many ways in which He demonstrated each. *"Patience is the great remedy from becoming panicky. To be able to use reason and good judgment when everyone else goes to pieces not only saves self, but also neighbor"* (Archbishop Fulton Sheen, Kelly, pg. 64).

By consciously increasing the virtues of humility and patience in our daily lives, they allow for a higher degree of the virtues of perseverance, endurance and strength. We need to consider how one has the ability to apply perseverance, endurance, and strength with an influential and intentional inner drive. Life experience can be a precursor to one's level of humility and patience. Having to withstand the crucible of being purified in many and very difficult trials and tribulations through life can quickly form humility and patience.

Fighting the chief sin of pride

Applying these virtues in a constant state demonstrates maturity and that one has acquired extraordinary resiliency. Curbing the content of one's comments and opinions can prevent gossip and slander. Patience and Humility excel at making someone slow to speak. This is good for our souls when we can douse the flames of pride. Remember that pride is probably the first or second sin I would guess that disgusts God the most. Arrogance and pride are what the devil showed in wanting to make himself God. Pride is that chief sin that formulates a base for many other sins. Let us practice humility and patience and use these pride extinguishing virtues against our ego and vanity.

We are born with a certain personality and character. Because of the world's influence and who we are subjected to live with or grow up around, we will have various degrees of humility and patience. We all know those people who are very sure of themselves despite their obvious shortcomings. There are those who put on an air of pride and an overbearing obnoxious quality of how they present themselves.

We also know people who are extremely impatient or short with others in their circumstances and situations. They demonstrate a quality of intolerance and can present themselves as annoyed with little and minor inconveniences. They are the opposite of content. Their irritability usually stems from inner disliking of themselves for one reason or another. Deep down they do not know why they are irked easily, but their aggravation is manifested in the way they treat others.

Understand that it is counterproductive to finding our purpose when one cannot display humility or patience. There are times when we slip and fall since we are human. Regarding those moments, we reflect on our actions and words and form a plan to not repeat them. For example, our feelings can get hurt and our pride offended when we learn of someone slandering us. The Lord taught one of our current modern-day mystics, (Ms. Vicky Smith, inonespirit.com, O Crux Ave Media) this concept. I paraphrase this thought that, *"One should not slander someone back, or slander the one who slandered us"*. This is a challenging and difficult action to refrain from wanting to defend ourselves or our reputation. One depletes their *"spiritual bank account"*, she went on to state when we slander or gossip.

On top of the slander, one needs to go to confession then to repent from this sin. The Lord loves us to be humble, and in our repentance, we receive graces. He is the one who will defend us when and if we truly need it. Additionally, to turn away from slander can be one of those previously mentioned sacrifices back to the Lord. This certainly takes a measure of humility.

Then there are others who do not acknowledge their own accomplishments or their strengths. These are people who are very quiet and patient without so much as a single complaint for conditions that could be considered very stressful or that pose a significant hardship in their lives. We all know or have encountered these personalities on both ends of the spectrum. The question is, when we truly and honestly evaluate our own selves, where do we fall within the continuum?

Our Lord's example

When we want to make the most of being a persevering, strong and enduring person we must evaluate how truly humble and patient we are. When we look at the best example the world can offer, we look back at Jesus's life and how he taught us to act. The level of perseverance, endurance, and strength that we can demonstrate and live depends upon having both virtues of humility and patience.

I often think of the times Jesus was spit upon. I am not sure I could have dealt with this very well. Then I think of how Jesus let it go and continued forward and I realize that was truly loving the other individual in the midst of hate. Let us look to our Lord's example first as we should in all things.

When we look at many examples of humility in the world we can once again reference the lives of the saints. Remember the definition of a saint. Saint simply means *"holy one"*. Our sainthood starts at Baptism and is fully realized once the soul gets to heaven or gets to their final dwelling place! In these examples, we are looking at those whom the Catholic Church has deemed true saints, or those we believe are in heaven. The saints in heaven are *"perfectly holy"* (Baltimore Catechism, 65-66). They learned from their Lord that by acquiring the virtue of humility, one can harness heavenly aid. The Lord loves the humble. Humility is emphasized consistently in many stories and verses in the bible.

To act the opposite of being pride-filled (which was the fault of Lucifer and the fallen angels, a.k.a. the devil) is to replicate the example of our Lord's humility. When we are humble, we recognize that all we are comes from God. He provides us with everything we have and all we need. While He gives us great gifts and talents, we use them for both ourselves, our families, and others. We demonstrate humility when we do not take an overabundance of credit for the good things we produce or accomplish. The virtue of humility is not something the worldly realm values. That is why God appreciates it when we are not prideful, but humble.

The humble person attracts others to their character

There is a draw, and inner desire to be close to the humble person. Their meekness and docility are qualities that others sense that make them stick out. People are magnetized to these types of personalities because they are refreshing, non-threatening, and desirable. These people attract others by their genuine and authentic personalities and do not put on a false character or airs. They are usually a very joyful and simple person who makes others feel at ease.

When one possesses humility and realizes all comes from the Lord, one becomes more willing to persevere, endure, and show strength in dealing with the challenges of life. One sometimes has to pray hard for the grace of obtaining this virtue. This means praying that one can have the help and grace to overcome pride. It can take an act of surrender to the Lord to exhibit humility. *"My child, perform your tasks with humility, then you will be loved by those whom God accepts, the greater you are, the more you must humble yourself; so you will find favor in the sight of the Lord."* (Sirach 3: 17-18).

When we look for an example of humility, we look to the one who created us. We look to the one who came to save us here on earth. The example of His life is portrayed in our four gospels, and the other New Testament authors uncover Jesus's true personality and character. If the one who holds all power and prestige, all knowledge and understanding, and the one who is immortal can be humble, it should go without question that we need to emulate this humility. It is not a bad thing to pray to become more like our Lord.

To be humble does not mean that one has to *"role over"* and be taken advantage of. It does not mean that one always be the last to receive good things. It does mean, however, that one weighs what is important and unimportant in worldly affairs compared to what matters significantly in our Lord's eyes.

For example, Jesus could have had kingdoms, riches, and all other sorts of pleasure and powers, but He declines without hesitation. Chronologically speaking, Jesus sets the devil straight right from the get go just before He begins His earthly ministry. We are told that Jesus was in the desert for 40 days and nights and that the evil one came to tempt Him there. Jesus immediately and completely rejects worshiping the devil. He also discards the temptation of worldly kingship and power, and yielding to needing worldly satisfactions of the body. Jesus, being the Son of God, could have demonstrated many of His powers and His Heavenly Kingship, but He is humble and deals directly with the enticements thrown at Him. He takes the badgering for a little while and then puts the devil in his place.

We can do the same thing while still remaining humble. We can call on Jesus when tempted. We can also call on our guardian angel to come to our defense in times of temptation. *"Jesus said to him, 'Away with you, Satan! For it is written, 'Worship the Lord your God, and serve only him". Then the devil left him and angels came and waited on him' (Matthew 4:10-11).* One has to understand not to engage the devil directly, but ask our Lord to vanquish the demons by His Holy Name. *"In the Holy Name of Jesus Christ, I command you to be gone away from me!"* We do not have the power, but the name of Jesus puts the demons to flight. We can also call upon our Holy Mother Mary. We are told by mystics that even a simple sigh from our Blessed Mother will send the demons flailing in retreat. This is because of Her great humility.

Other examples of true humility

St. Therese of Lisieux, a Doctor of the Church (meaning she was elevated to the title of "Doctor of the Church" in the Catholic Church) as one who made significant contribution to the Church's theology and teachings, was also known as the *"Little Flower"*. She relied on God in total abandonment to His providence. She therefore developed an extraordinary humility and one that she tried to share. Her *"little"*, or somewhat seemingly insignificant actions by the way she lived, helped define who she was in her relationship to God. A type of relationship that we need to develop if we want to come closer to God. She was so favored by God that today she is a very popular saint, and one whom others try hard to emulate. She put up with many sufferings and sacrifices and did so with humility and patience. She died at the age of 24, but in that time, she became a virtue powerhouse.

The reason we mention this is because one needs to have this degree of humility since God expects it. Sometimes it can only come through a deep and intense desire to become humble and rely on God fully. St. Therese mentions in a prayer God's expectancy for us. *"Lord, I recognize how weak I am, but every day I recognize in my weakness an occasion for salutary (confidence). You deign to impart to me the wisdom which makes me 'glory in my infirmities'. This is a very great grace. In it I find peace and rest for my heart. I have now learned to know your 'character': You give as being God, but you expect from us humility"* (Van de Putte, pg. 183). In this state of mind, one also has to take on in our humility, childlike qualities and truly count on God to provide for our needs. This can really help us to persevere, endure and be strong with whatever life throws at us.

Humility is the opposite of pride. Pride was the reason for the angels fall from grace

It is so important to develop and grow in humility. We too need to become childlike in our loving, obedience and confidence in God's providence. It goes against ambition to be self-reliant when we rely on God's providential ways. It is for our own good, but difficult to sometimes just sit back and let Him provide. He wants us to be child-like to fight against the number one sin in the world which is pride. Jesus understands this and comes right out and tells us that unless we develop this spiritual childlike nature, that we cannot obtain heaven. *"I assure you, unless you change and become like little children, you will not enter the Kingdom of God" (Mt 18:2-3).*

Satan and his fallen cohort would not embrace the idea that they needed God. They would rather call themselves gods. It, however, cost them heaven forever. Yes forever! We do not want to make the same mistake. Our job is to recognize that while we go through all these struggles and challenges, we develop this humility by asking for it and practicing it until it is our nature to be humble.

God sees our desire to please Him and is actually more willing to help us out when we surrender to His Will for us. This surrender requires patience, however, as prayers are not always immediately answered as we have discussed. It is something we need to pray and maybe even fast for to acquire these graces. Fasting is something we will talk about more, but it is a discipline that shows God we are serious. Here is a very difficult prayer for some. When prayed time to time, however, God has no choice but to provide us with what we need to become childlike. Let us pray this Litany of Humility.

O Jesus! Meek and humble of heart, **h*ear Me.***

From the desire of being esteemed,
From the desire of being loved,
From the desire of being extolled,
From the desire of being honored,
From the desire of being praised,
From the desire of being preferred,
From the desire of being consulted,
From the desire of being approved,

Deliver me Jesus.
From the fear of being humiliated,
From the fear of being despised,
From the fear of suffering rebukes,
From the fear of being calumniated,
From the fear of being forgotten,
From the fear of being ridiculed,
From the fear of being wronged,
From the fear of being suspected,

Deliver me Jesus.
That others may be loved more than I,
That others may be esteemed more than I,
That in the opinion of the world, others may increase, and I may decrease,
That others may be chosen and I set aside,
That others may be praised and I unnoticed,
That others may be preferred to me in everything,
That others become holier than I, provided that I may become as holy as I should,
Jesus, grant me the grace to desire it.
(Pieta Prayer Book, 2001).

Patience will spare you much worry in life

In the same fashion, the more one can develop the virtue of patience and display this to others, the more one is able to persevere, endure, and be strong. Patience might mean learning not to have the last word in a tense discussion. Patience might take the form of being calm when society makes others feel apprehension and worry. Patience could be in the appearance of being joyful and in harmony with the way things are, while knowing that things will eventually change for the better. In any regard, one needs to develop patience as well.

Praying for patience is something I believe the Lord appreciates and delivers upon; however, He allows us to be cognizant of working more towards being patient. In other words, we have to coach ourselves to be patient at times. St. Paul prayed for the Colossians to acquire this virtue all the while giving thanks to God for allowing them to bear through struggles and sufferings. *"May you be made strong with all the strength that comes from his glorious power, and may you be prepared to endure everything with patience, while joyfully giving thanks to the Father, who has enabled you to share in the inheritance of the saints in the light. He has rescued us from the power of darkness and transferred us into the kingdom of his beloved Son, in whom we have redemption, the forgiveness of sins" (Colossians 1: 11-14).*

Again, looking at our Lord Jesus's patience, we can point to many examples where He displayed extravagant patience with us. His most profound example of patience was no doubt understanding that He was to teach, heal, and demonstrate the love He had for others over three years-time. He demonstrated this patience the whole while knowing that those closest to Him would turn, desert, and betray Him. He was tortured and killed for the sake of the world all the while displaying incredible patience. This virtue is no doubt a quality of our Lord's inmost being. For that reason alone, it is therefore a worthwhile virtue to be desired and sought after in our own right. This is the *"seeking"* of heavenly things versus worldly things to want to have these virtues in this life. *"Set your minds on things that are above, not on things that are on earth," (Colossians 3:2).*

Patience is a gift of the Holy Spirit

For those who do not know this, patience is a *"fruit"* or a gift from the Holy Spirit. The Catholic Church teaches that patience is something that is a gift from the Holy Spirit and a great gift it is. When speaking of these fruits, Fr. Paul O'Sullivan states this in his book *The Holy Ghost our Greatest Friend, "These graces are called "Fruits" because they are crowning favors, the result of all the Holy Spirit has been doing for us. They are to our souls what the fruit is to the tree". (pg. 24)*. It is imperative to call on the Holy Spirit to gain these graces, these fruits.

I would be remiss not to tie in a very important aspect of patience in the concept that the Blessed Virgin Mary (mine and your Heavenly Mother, also referred to as Our Lady) is considered to be the Holy

Spirit's spouse. She is the one that God chose to become the mother of the Savior of the world. Only one person was chosen for this! If she was that important to God, then she should be that much more significant to us in our own lives. Call on the Blessed Virgin Mary to teach us patience and humility.

Get the Blessed Mother Mary to help you acquire humility and patience

It behooves anyone to request the assistance of a mother when times get difficult. Reaching out and asking Our Lady to pray for us, that is to say, "*Please intercede for us to the Holy Spirit*", amplifies the call we make to God the Third Person in acquiring these graces and fruits. She is very powerful in that She is the mother of our Lord Jesus as He chose Her from all other women. Scripture tells us that the Archangel Gabriel identified Her as a Favored daughter of God. *"Greetings , favoured one! The Lord is with you." (Luke 1:28).* She is both the epitome of humility and patience, and learning from Her example is a remarkable and insightful gift. God chose Her to dispense many graces, and She wants a relationship with us as previously discussed. Do not be afraid to invoke Her assistance in acquiring these virtues.

Think of this as a profound statement in and of itself. To be named the Mother of God is no less than awe-inspiring, tremendous, and astounding. She is exceedingly significant in our lives to the extent we allow Her to act and honor Her role in the plan for salvation. We honor Her, however, but do not worship Her. This is an important distinction, and one in which many accuse Catholics of doing. The Blessed Mother is still a creature made by God, but one whom He chose for His own mom. Jesus called this lady "Mommy". He loved Her and respected Her until His last breath.

Therefore, learn to reach out to the Blessed Virgin Mary, and be assured that She will come to your assistance and fast! She will help you acquire these gifts of patience and humility so that you can become closer to Her Son Jesus and ultimately to heaven. As a little side bonus, when you call on Her to ward off the demons, they cannot stand Her holiness and flee as soon as She is invoked. Our Mother will come to your rescue. Develop a relationship with her today.

She is not a lackadaisical mother. She is very active and waits for a person to recognize Her Queenship. She waits for the day that you concede and realize that you are Her spiritual child. An adopted brother or sister of Her Son the King. That technically makes you royalty. Did you know you were heavenly royalty? The Queen of the Universe wants you to ask Her for assistance.

If you do not yet know Her or are unsure if what I state to be true, then please dare to request the following for a short period of time. Take the chance as it is absolutely risk free. It is totally worth investing a small period of invocation to Her.

Say this short prayer for ten days, two or three times a day, and you are guaranteed to start a relationship with Her. If you are genuine and authentic in your intentions, She will reveal Herself to you. *"Dear Blessed Mother, Our Holy help, please reveal yourself to me!"* She will introduce Herself. You will feel Her love for you. It is nice to have a heavenly mother as your super advocate. We form this relationship as She is our advocate to Jesus, and helps us to live a virtuous and holy life. We rely on the Blessed Mother to help us get to our heavenly dwelling place.

One additional thought with the idea of patience is this. When you ask this from our Mother Mary, you can ask Her for a portion of Her patience as well. Think of all She had to suffer, endure, and persevere through watching and experiencing firsthand Her Holy Son being ridiculed, falsely accused, condemned, tortured, crucified, mocked on the cross, and finally innocently dying all because of humanity's sins. Your sin and mine. She is the human personification of patience. This is why

She is favored by our Lord as Queen of the Universe. Having Her on your side means gaining the most powerful ally to heaven. When the Queen asks for something on your behalf, the King makes it come to fruition.

Here is one last thought on being humble and reaching out to the Blessed Virgin Mary for help. Devotion to Her and asking for Her assistance to make oneself worthy before God is a great humility. One can gain God's help the more one develops the virtue of humility. Gaining God's help can certainly make taking on tasks that require perseverance and endurance much less strenuous.

Take recommendation from a Saint who understood that humbling oneself was actually self-serving and very wise in the long run. St. Louis De Montfort states this exact advice regarding devotion to the Blessed Mother to help us show our gratitude to God. We acknowledge ourselves unworthy to approach His majesty and ask our Mother for Her intervention. *"Moreover, this devotion is a practice of great humility, which God loves above all other virtues. A soul which exalts itself abases God; a soul which abases itself exalts God. God resists the proud and gives His grace to the humble....Oh how He loves humility of heart!" (True Devotion to Mary, pages 90-91).*

This is only a suggestion if you happen to look inside yourself and determine the need for a humbler character. Often there is a prompting, a suggestion from the Holy Spirit. It eventually weighs on your mind and heart to become humbler.

God the Father shows us His own patience

Finally, let's not forget God the Father's patience with mankind. We learn from God's example in the development of our own patience. I think of all the times that one personally sins and knows that it was probably something God would not approve. Yet, for whatever pressure, stress, or desire we commit the sin anyway. I think of all times God could have let us drown in our sin, or could have not supported our lives. Yet, He upholds His end of the bargain by sustaining our lives. He gives us every chance to convert our lives back to Him. Sometimes He waits 80 years or so before He calls us to give an account of our faithfulness and love for one another and Him. Sometimes it is not that long, but we have to try and appreciate the idea of being patient with others as He is patient with us.

He does not will to destroy us or have us go to hell. We, by our actions and will either choose heaven or hell. He wants us to repent and reform and to choose Him. He is willing to allow this gradually and work with us, because He knows we are bombarded and tormented by the enemy.

He factors all this in during our lives and is fair and faithful. His patience is synonymous with His Divine Mercy. *"But you are merciful to all, for you can do all things, and you over look people's sins, so they may repent. For you love all things that exist, and detest none of the things that you have made, for you would not have made anything if you had hated it. How would anything have endured if you had not willed it? Or how would anything not called for by you have been preserved? You spare all things, for they are yours, O Lord, you who love the living. For your immortal spirit is in all things. Therefore, you correct little by little those who trespass, and you remind and warn them of the things through which they sin, so that they may be freed from wickedness and put their trust in you, O Lord"* (The Wisdom of Solomon, 11: 23 -26, 12: 1-2). Thank you for your great and wonderful patience with me, God and Father. Help me to become worthy of this enormous gift of your patience with me! Help me to get to my dwelling place.

CHAPTER SEVEN

The Prerequisite Virtues: Courage, Hope, Faith, and Love

Virtues are interwoven and support each other's implementation

Without overanalyzing things, there is a need to connect for the reader and explain that virtues build upon one another, overlap, and are interwoven. We reviewed how humility and patience are structural virtues that help grow perseverance, endurance, and strength. Yes, virtues can either complement and grow other virtues, or lack thereof can diminish volume and quality of virtue.

When we think of what helps us grow and exhibit perseverance, endurance, and strength, we learned that humility and patience support and edify us in the sense that these provide a sort of booster chair for our demeanor and behavior. Humility and patience give us a foundation to display strength, perseverance, and endurance. This happens first by choosing to implement humility and patience as basic self-control virtues that eventually combine with the latter virtues as time and experience matures one's self-will. The latter three higher self-disciplining virtues are then executed and purposely practiced when one becomes cognizant of one's own mental willpower. When willpower is discovered, it then allows them to then apply these three virtues accordingly to the situation. In this instance, I would argue that discipline is a virtue that is developed in the process. While we are not studying discipline so much in this writing, I would make the case that it bridges the gap between humility and patience and perseverance, strength, and endurance. You can now perhaps see how these virtues support each other.

If we can just spend a moment in discussing the following virtues of courage (we can refer to this in certain instances as the virtue of fortitude), hope, faith and love, we can also tie in these great virtues to see that again, certain virtues can nurture, cultivate, and increase the others. It is when all these are encompassed and utilized that one is definitively growing in holiness.

We learned earlier that the devil will do all things to keep us from Jesus. Be encouraged to know that when you are struggling with finding faith, or being charitable (loving someone), or are at a loss for hope, that often it is evil that is thwarting our efforts. It is then we call on our Lord outright and rebuke the evil that threatens our daily joyfulness and trust. It is then that we are being purified and made more faithful because we never give up. It soon becomes easier to deal with whatever situation arises.

Remember that we started off this book with the intent to raise to the forefront that one has a very important purpose in life. We discussed that sometimes one needs to enhance and rely upon our virtuous living to ultimately put into perspective and get to the point where one sees and recognizes the purpose for one's life. We then looked to the most perfect example of the God who created us, and Jesus the one who eternally saves us. The idea was to point out, contemplate, honor and worship Jesus because of the sum of His example. He showed us the way to take on trials and hardships in this world.

Now we look to Him again to have the reader understand that these virtues of courage, hope, faith, and love (sometimes also referred to as charity) are prerequisite virtues that grow and multiply the more one seasons and expands the love one has for God. These four virtues are criteria for the necessity of being "*children of the light*". (Luke 16 : 8). We belong to God because He is light and not darkness. We have to have these as basics before being able to show signs of perseverance, endurance, and strength.

Love is the greatest of all virtues

Let us consider what St. Paul says regarding what love is. In the first Letter to the Corinthians, (people of Corinth in the first century A.D., or anno Domini, or anno Domini nostril Jesu Christi, or in the year of our Lord), (Transitions by the Book, www.Transistionbythebook.com), where in one of his ministerial journeys to various areas, this one of modern-day southern Greece, he spells things out for the people and for us. He tells us what the definition of love is. Why do I mention anno Domini? This is to provide even more confidence to the reader that even people two-thousand years ago recognized Jesus's influence on history. The world and its calendar changed. They started a new era that we recognize as the time when our Lord physically was present here on earth. This gives us even more assuredness that others recognized our God then. They recognized Jesus as true love for all He went through.

St. Paul outlines for us that great gifts and even spiritual endowments that one may possess do not amount to much if one is lacking love. He says the following: 1 Corinthians chapter 13, *"If I speak in the tongues of mortals and of angels, but do not have love, I am a noisy gong or a clanging cymbal. And if I have prophetic powers, and understand all mysteries and all knowledge, and if I have all faith so as to remove mountains, but do not have love, I am nothing. If I give away all my possessions, and if I hand over my body so that I may boast, but do not have love, I gain nothing."* He is telling us that we have to be able to love and show love before the other virtues can be of benefit to us. We have to have love like Jesus did to be able to do greater things that help us get to heaven. The other virtues we put into practice after empowering love in our lives are ways we grow in holiness. These are ways we show God we are heartfelt in the love we offer Him. St. Paul is saying that a person can pray for the gift of love to be given us.

Then he goes on to delineate exactly what love is*: "Love is patient; love is kind; love is not envious or boastful or arrogant or rude. It does not* *insist on its own way; it is not irritable or resentful; it does not rejoice in wrongdoing, but rejoices in the truth. It bears all things, believes all things, hopes all things, endures all things. Love never ends." (1 Corin. 13: 4-8).* I do not want to speak for everyone reading this, but it certainly serves me especially well to hear this passage from St. Paul often. It comforts one to understand love, but convicts us to demonstrate love as labeled. It points all the more to the way Jesus acts towards us and how He cares and respects us. Do you think you show love as designated above? Do you always express your love for others in these terms? I find hope in the fact that love never ends!

Virtuous living

We are learning this construct by repeating the idea that virtues comfort us. Virtuous living lends a hand in allowing us to have a flourishing search to find that ultimate reason for existing. We learned that commitment or single-mindedness is to live life to know, love, and serve God on our way to the heavenly home. We need to look at this final home as our true mansion and future estate.

I think it is safe to say we are going to have a very prosperous and thriving place to exist with our heavenly family and friends. How easy is it to forget that we are living in a place that is our temporary home. Earth alone is not our final residence. One needs to be courageous to persevere and endure to this final residence. Bourgeoning a love for others assists us in implementing our strength to overcome those sufferings and sacrifices encountered here in the present. These sufferings and sacrifices deprived us at the time of comforts, security, and joyfulness, but we proved our love. Our love blossoms hope and faith that God is trustworthy. By these sufferings and sacrifices, our reward will be even better!

When we learn we can adapt and acclimate, adjust and modify, bend without breaking, and smile versus becoming hateful, we are demonstrating all these virtues put together. When we learn to ask God to increase in us courage, hope, faith (really faith can be also defined as trust and belief), and love, He will do so. When we have an ample dose of these virtues, one can stand firm in and speak to oneself about having the ability to fight and battle with evil each day. Jesus gives us copious amounts of grace to overcome evil at all times. It is up to us to focus on this grace and keep our eyes fixed on Jesus.

Let us contemplate the grace He gives us. He gives us grace, but we need to be open to and ask for more grace before it is given to us. What is grace really? Vicky Smith identifies grace as "*supernatural help*" (inonespirit.com). This is supernatural power from heaven to sufficiently overcome evil temptation and taunts. This grace spiritually delivers us from evil and gives us fortitude to strive to become more like God in love and charity. Vicky Smith, when talking about this spiritual engagement, (more accurately spiritual warfare), that we are not to say the term "spiritual warfare" in a sentence without including the fact that one will have "Victory" in the name of Jesus. In other words, when we speak of the reality that we engage in spiritual warfare with the evil one, we must be assured that we will be victorious when we call on Jesus to protect us, fight for us, and win the war for us. Here is a portion of a prayer that binds up evil spirits who are working against us. *"In the Holy Name of Jesus, I claim Victory over and I break and dissolve any and all curses, hexes, spells, snares, traps, lies, obstacles, deceptions, diversions, spiritual influences, evil wishes, evil desires, hereditary seals, known and unknown, and every dysfunction and disease from any source including my mistakes and sins." (Paraphrased, H.O.M. Ministries).*

Take back what is yours, the victory is already won with Jesus!

Make no mistake that we are in a battle for our souls, the souls of our families, and that of our other adopted brothers and sisters. For those of us that are competitive, let this character become another strength in you. Become aggressive in the fact that it is your soul, and that it does not belong to evil who has done nothing but abuse and deter your life. Your soul belongs to the One that created you and loves you. This you demonstrate by your willingness to viably fight back. So, let us pursue our Lord and emulate and copy Jesus when it comes to phenomena we have to confront. *"The Holy Spirit wants to strengthen all the areas of our being, and since all these areas work together, if there is something blocking any one area, other areas suffer" (Petrisko, pg. 115).* Let us request of the Holy Spirit to then strengthen our being. Let the Holy Spirit reveal any areas in your life that you have allowed Satan to have a foothold in your life. Break these ties and bonds by asking Jesus to sever these oppressions.

Let us look at an example of courage and more so fortitude (as this mainly refers to courage in the midst of much pain and/or adversity). No one can refute that our Lord did not give us an example of courage. When Jesus was in the garden of Gethsemane, He knew that in a few hours He would be put to death on a cross. He even sweat blood because He knew the pain He was to endure. This is actually a real-life medical condition for some. It is called hematidrosis, or sweating blood. It is linked to intense emotional or physical stress, such as extreme fear. Jesus actually had this happen to Him because of what our sins were going to cost Him. "Praise You Lord! Thank you for bravely withstanding the cost of my sinfulness!"

The biggest act of courage, however, was when He faced an angry mob of soldiers and temple Jews that were sent to arrest Him. Some mystics say there were approximately 300-600 people in this mob that came for Him that late evening on Holy Thursday. Imagine having that many people come for you knowing full well what they came to do. For one person? You know the evil one was behind all this.

Who do you think is behind mobs and violent protests these days as well? I give our Lord honor and glory for still going through with His suffering after that moment. It is one of the single most courageous acts of all to demonstrate and tell them at the same time that He was God when He said *"I Am"* to Judas and his group, and then hand Himself over to the wolfpack. *"Then Jesus, knowing all that was to happen to him, came forward and asked them, 'For whom are you looking?' They answered, 'Jesus of Nazareth.' Jesus replied, 'I am he.' Judas, who betrayed him, was standing with them. When Jesus said to them 'I am he', they stepped back and feel to the ground."* (John 18: 4-6). The next time you have to admit to a mistake, or the need of courage to step forward, or the necessity to defend someone knowing there will be retaliation or consequence, quickly recall this scene from history. You will gain the nerve to do what is proper. You will be able to muster the guts to advance headlong into the conflict. Jesus will be there if you call on Him to help you. "Jesus, I trust in You!"

Hope and Courage

Thinking then of a time when both hope and faith were demonstrated in the life of Jesus, there is a dramatic incident. It was an amazing and thought-provoking spectacle that most could not see coming the first time they heard the story. I am speaking about the interchange between Jesus and the good thief, while both hanging on their respective crosses. Some may know the good thief as Dismas. Early historical accounts remind us of this being his name. If you recollect, the crucifixion of our Lord also included two thieves, "*criminals*" the bible text tells us, *"one on His right and the other on the left".* (Luke 23:33). In an act of enormous faith after learning who Jesus was, with a last-ditch effort of impressively vast hope, Dismas pleads before Jesus's Divine Mercy and asks to be remembered. In other words, he asks Jesus to be forgiven and saved. Jesus responds to the reverent faith and hope that Dismas remarkably exhibits at the most critical of times. It just shows that we can invoke our Lord at any time in our lives with the same hope and faith. What God returns, even if at the last second, is Divine Love and Mercy. Can you think of another faith and hope scenario that holds more proof of God's love for us?

There are others examples (maybe when Abraham was about to sacrifice his only son Issac) that are probably on the same plane, but this paradigm stands out regarding those two virtues. "*One of the criminals who were hanged there kept deriding him and saying, 'Are you not the Messiah? Save yourself and us!' But the other rebuked him, saying, 'Do you not fear God, since you are under the same sentence of condemnation? And we indeed have been condemned justly, for we are getting what we deserve for our deeds, but this man has done nothing wrong.' Then he said, 'Jesus, remember me when you come into your kingdom.' He replied, 'Truly I tell you, today you will be with me in Paradise'* (Luke 23:39-43). Dismas secured for himself, through this act of hope and faith in Jesus, the right to be one of the first citizens of heaven. Talk about believing the right thing at the right time! It is a warranted example in the unfailing Mercy of Jesus. This was truly a historical display that Jesus left us to ponder and consider for our own wretchedness. All we have to do is be sincerely sorry and ask forgiveness.

The ultimate relationship with our Father

Finally, when we think of the virtue of love, we can point to no greater example than the extremely hopeful example of the love of God our Father. The Father created us because He wants to have a relationship with us. Think of the best relationships in your life and how much you enjoy or have enjoyed them. Then try to fathom a relationship with God. The reason God wants this relationship is that He wants us to know and seek Him. He wants us to find out more about who He is. It is this curiosity in God that develops our love for an eternity. It is natural for us to desire those whom we love to know us.

We have to do two things to merit this creation and adoption as a son or daughter. The first is fairly easy. The second is the hard part and the reason the information is written down for you. The first is that God loved us so much, that He sent His Son Jesus to come to our rescue and free us from the sin of our first parents. This meant that He had to rescue us from the wages of sin which is death. This is referred to as redemption as we learned earlier. When we believe in Jesus and what He did for us we can claim salvation from hell, or eternal punishment by choosing to do God's will as we also ascertained. *"And just as Moses lifted up the serpent in the wilderness, so must the Son of Man be lifted up, that whoever believes in him may have eternal life. 'For God so loved the world that he gave his only Son, so that everyone who believes in him may not perish but may have eternal life"* (John 3: 14-16). Thank you, Holy Trinity for caring for us!

The second part of this meriting is doing God's will. This is where we find purpose in life, because we want to please Him, and in so doing, we find happiness, fulfillment, and joy. We find the most contentment we can in this earthly existence. We then live to do God's will. We live to become that royal red cedar in whatever form God has designed for our lives. We purposefully demonstrate and exemplify those same characteristics that Christ taught us to display and form. This is the hard part. However, our perseverance, endurance, and strength given to us through our prayer and desire for God can get us to this reality. It is certainly not merely idealism when one considers all that is included in developing virtue.

The Will of the Father

The Gospel according to St. Matthew helps us out here. *"Not everyone who says to me "Lord, Lord", will enter the kingdom of heaven, but only one who does the will of my Father in heaven. (Matthew, 7:21).* Notice something here? You have to actually fulfill what is asked of you, and all of us are asked something different to accomplish. You cannot only say you will undertake something, but it must be demonstrated, and most often, more than once in life.

It is hard to do the will of the Father because you are in the middle of a test. Worse yet, you sometimes have to search it out, and discern what that will might be. The good news is that it is summarized in doing good, being merciful, and acting upright and justly despite what the world tells us. What God calls you to do is ultimately a discernment process that you do your best to fulfill. This can be very difficult and hence is why we need to be persevering, enduring and strong. Prayers and supplications to God to reveal to you what He wants are very necessary. *"He has told you O mortal, what is good; and what does the Lord require of you but to do justice, and to love kindness, and to walk humbly with God? (Micha 6:8).* Does any of this sound familiar with what we are discussing, with anything we have been shown from Jesus? *"For it is God's will that by doing right, you should silence the ignorance of the foolish" 1 Peter 2:15.*

Let us then learn to love, to hope, to have faith, and courage. These foundational and bedrock virtues come as gifts from the Holy Spirit. We again need to pray for each virtue to be increased in us. When we sacrifice and suffer, we offer them to God and He multiplies the grace. He gives us an abundance of that supernatural help we need, because we have made an effort to invest that grace as first deposits of ourselves back towards Him. We demonstrate and reciprocate that love that He shows us. *"And now faith, hope, and love abide, these three; and the greatest of these is love."* (1 Corinthians 13: 13).

CHAPTER EIGHT

Resiliency and the Aroma of Joy

No question that suffering makes us tough

It is time to talk about some of the fruits and benefits of endurance and suffering. It is a gift that one is allowed to suffer. It is said to us from the saints that the angels wish they could suffer like man does, because the merits of suffering have great rewards in heaven. They are also a gift back to God. That should tell us something about the significance of suffering well, and why Jesus suffered.

This means that if we use these sufferings wisely, many things are "banked up" for us in heaven. Suffering then takes on a new meaning for us in our overall perspective on life. *Resiliency* is defined as, "*the ability to successfully adapt to stressors, maintaining psychological well-being in the face of adversity.*" It is the ability to adapt and bounce back from adversity, trauma, or stressful situations. How does one obtain this resiliency? By making it a value in one's mind that notion of how to persevere, endure, and become strong. By fostering and cherishing these three virtues that we are contemplating and trying to understand better, they inherently become part of our ingrained character. In other words, we strive to make the virtues common place as to acquire more and more resiliency. We ask Jesus to make us even stronger in our abilities and daily living.

Let us backtrack and revisit our red cedar analogy. Juniperus Virginiana. We discussed that one of the best qualities of the red cedar is that it fights natural decay and rot to a very high level. It is that same rot and deterioration that often befall other trees exposed to the same elements. We compare our lives to the lives of others and how we try to avoid the decay of the worldly elements.

We need to strive to acquire these virtues so we can have an inner quality that naturally keeps us from rotting away on the inside to all the contaminants with which society and the world continue to entice and paralyze us with. We develop this resiliency as an antidote to the poison venoms that can interiorly cause us to have our virtues putrefy and decompose. The virtues are remedies. When practiced, these are cures that keep our soul and conscience from becoming disintegrated on the inside. We gain this resiliency inasmuch as we continue to practice virtue as opposed to practicing wickedness.

I find that the species name for the red cedar "Virginiana" to be not so much a coincidence when I think of the Virgin Mary. She too was incorrupt and pure, wholesome and full, fresh and solid, and aromatic with a heavenly scent. Do you know that when She manifests Her presence from heaven on earth that the smell is often like lilacs? It is true that sometimes people are chosen by heaven to be visited and heaven brings them messages. These visitations are referred to as apparitions. They take some time to be authenticated by the Catholic Church. However, the ones that are deemed true, produce great graces.

The Blessed Mother provides an example of the sweet fragrance of joy

I certainly would not say "no" to an encounter with our heavenly Mother. She is not in any way irrelevant to our lives. Her ability to express and display these virtues, especially strength, is very much Christ-like. I think of the fact that She did not become desolate and despairing even though exposed to the ultimate desolation upon losing Her only son. I, on the other hand, would likely demonstrate a salty, bitter, sarcastic, and probably hateful attitude towards God if I had lost a child. It would take much grace not to lose faith. Yet, She displays Her strength as the stories go by continuing to steer the apostles back to their mission. She somehow joyfully moved the Church, (and is still moving the Church), forward with Her qualities and unique "aroma". That aroma given off by Her very nature as She is that providential red cedar example from God for us.

By demonstrating these virtues and acquiring these red cedar-like qualities, we acquire a gift from God in becoming resilient to the world's abuse, to the world's neglect for love, and thus resilient to interior decay. We are able to not only tolerate hardships and unfavorable instances in our lives, but flourish and overcome many obstacles. All because we asked God to help and were willing to change our inner-self.

Is it now obvious that we can then more purposefully fulfill God's will by acquiring the resilience necessary for us to take things head on? You become that beautiful and steadfast cedar tree that can withstand the rain, sleet, snow and scorching heat. You now miraculously possess that inner quality that fights degeneration and rotting that can come from the toxic chemicals the world feeds us each day because of the virtues you now display and possess. These are the virtues you were shown and given by Jesus and His Father. These proved to overcome the toxic pollutants that would otherwise continue to corrode and crumble our spiritual, physical, mental and emotional selves. Thank you for incrementally changing us to be more like you, Lord!

If resiliency is a fruit produced by practicing virtues, sacrifices and enduring suffering, what fruit does resiliency generate? We discussed above a sweet-smelling aroma associated with the Virgin Mary, one that we can reflect in ourselves. One that attracts others. Because of an upright and virtuous lifestyle, your very essence can exude a fragrant smell that others notice. People can sense the natural goodness that comes from your spirit. Resiliency produced in an overall holy and good regiment in turn yields much productivity, and joy that others want to be around. This type of person is so attractive to God and to other people that your example and way of life then become contagious. It is this goodness that is something highly sought after and looked for by others.

Joy deflects worry and anxiety

It was said of St. Mother Theresa that she treated everyone with such dignity and respect that many commented that she made individuals feel as if they were the most prominent person in the world. Mother Theresa, when asked about this, (and I am paraphrasing), stated, *Everyone has Jesus inside them. I strive to see Jesus in that person and care for them as if it were Jesus.* Mother Theresa worked with the poorest of the poor, and was resilient to all impediments in caring for these people. Mother Theresa was joyful and smiling all the time. People were naturally attracted to her goodness. The focus was on others and not herself. Let us strive to see Jesus in others and produce this joy from which others highly benefit.

When you fashion and produce these virtues in your life, you earn and acquire the opportunity and right to be an aromatic cedar full of joy with the ability to overcome high winds and storms with a smile. Your joyfulness, and with inner peace is something that no one can highjack from you. This joy overcomes daily worries. This joyous presence amidst the harshness in the world is a delight for the heavenly Father. He sees His invaluable creation and all that you have formidably gone through to do His will in doing good and enduring much suffering. He sees your humility. We are then reminded He loves the humble servant. Strive to be that red cedar and your saintly scent will reach his throne in the highest heaven. *"The righteous flourish like the palm tree, and grow like a cedar in Lebanon. They are planted in the house of the Lord; they flourish in the courts of our God. In old age they still produce fruit; they are always green and full of sap, showing that the Lord is upright; his is my rock, and there is no unrighteous in him". (Psalm 92: 12-15).*

CHAPTER NINE

A Higher Reality of Love and Endurance

Jesus shows us a higher reality

I want to gently challenge the reader to mull over both love and endurance to an even higher level of reality. This should really put things into perspective for us if we have never contemplated in totality Jesus's sacrifice. When we think of the Lord Jesus's suffering in all its facets, I am ashamed at my sinfulness and ignorance of His love for me. When men and women are in love with one another, they would give their lives for one another as an expression of their love and as a sacrifice if required. Jesus created the Church. The analogy and mystical reality to this fact is that He is the Church's Bridegroom and the Church is His Bride. The Church meaning all those who have entered into the true faith.

It is possible to be members of this Church insomuch as one enters the Catholic faith through the sacraments and becomes part of this Church. We are therefore espoused to Christ through the mystery of the Church. Christ died for His Church. He underwent all suffering and sacrifice for you and I.

There are a few more significant particulars that require dissecting in order to put into perspective that which will make you desire to live the remainder of your life for Christ. Let me say I appreciate and recognize that some of those reading this writing are at an unprecedented time of suffering in their lives. Your life is almost unbearable. One cannot take much more of life's abuse and mistreatment. It is precisely now when you need to get on your knees, literally, and say to Jesus, *"Please enter into this massive issue Lord! This is excruciating and agonizing, and*

I cannot endure much more!" This is a cry of despair before despondency sets in. I am telling you that Jesus, the Divine Physician, will come to mend your broken spirit and provide healing relief.

There are still others that have already experienced and lived through unsurpassed difficult times. These individuals are still endeavoring to deal with things as they come. This might be another chapter in your life, that still requires Jesus to enter in and heal significant trauma wounds. Either way, please allow me to propose to you comfort in pondering and taking to heart what I am about to have you learn. This might be the first time or at least be a reminder to you of the deep love Jesus has for us. It is not too late to call on His Divine providence. There is no one throughout history who has suffered more than our Lord. For this reason, He can relate and restore all injuries and sorrows. Please consider this:

It is stated that St. Elizabeth of Hungary, St. Matilda, and St. Bridgit, (and I know others such as Blessed Ann Catherine Emerich) were privileged to know how much our Lord suffered for us during His passion. By their fervent prayers they were allowed to know many fine details of our Lord's own suffering and sacrifice. The following are the details of how much He persevered and endured for us:

Please consider the words our Lord spoke to these saints in the following manner: Our Lord said *"Be it known that the number of armed soldiers were 150; those who trailed Me while I was bound were 23. The executioners of justice were 83; the blows received on my head were 150; those on My stomach, 108; kicks on My shoulders, 80; I was led, bound with cords, by the hair, 24 times; spits in the face were 180; I was beaten on the body, 6666 times; beaten on the head, 110 times. I was roughly pushed, and at 12 o'clock was lifted up by the hair; pricked with thorns and pulled by the beard, 23 times; received 20 wounds on the head; thorns of marine junks, 72; pricks of thorns in the head 110; mortal thorns in the forehead, 3; I was afterwards flogged and dressed as a mocked king; wounds in the body, 1000; The soldiers who led Me to the Calvary were 608; those who watched Me were 3, and those who mocked me were 1008; the drops of blood which I lost were 28,430.* (Benedetta DA S.S., Pope Leo XIII H. In Roma, April 5, 1890, From the Pieta Prayer Book).

This is not even considering what He endured in the Garden of Gethsemane, and through the interrogation of the High Priest after the agony in the Garden in the early hours of the morning. Does this not take strength, endurance, and perseverance to an all-time high? Wait! There is more to be considered here regarding our Lord's lived out mental and physical anguish.

Very few people deal well with being forcibly pinned down. Most panic and become claustrophobic when one's hands, arms, feet and legs are rendered immovable for whatever reason. Reflect and meditate what compares to having your hands and arms secured and immobilized after having them nailed in place and your wrists wrapped to a beam of lumber. I dare say that nothing compares to this helpless and horrible feeling.

The thought of full restrain makes me hold my breath and start feeling the desperation of suffocation. It is said that Jesus's shoulder was pulled out of the socket by the Roman soldiers while nailing him to the cross. Can you imagine bearing weight all that time on a dislocated shoulder? The other shoulder had a wound so bad that Jesus describes this as His most painful wound that was not recorded by men but by St. Bernard of Clairvaux.

Imagine having the flies bite your face and skin so painfully and not being able to brush them off or recover by rubbing your skin? Can you sense having back aches and pains from being in such an uncomfortable position? Can you relate to having all your weight on the inner parts and muscles of your feet after the metatarsal bones in your feet were already spread apart by the large nails? Can you illustrate in your mind this open flesh being the support for the body weight especially after being flogged to an unrecognizable bloody body? Then, consider the inability to release your feet and move your legs for hours and hours. Then your consciousness becomes numb. *"MY DEAR LORD*

AND MY GOD, HAVE MERCY ON MY SINFULNESS! I am so sorry for putting you in this unspeakable set of circumstances!"

Reconsider God's love for us

The reason the author brings this to the reader's attention is to emphasize God's love for us. Often times we hear people say, *"I cannot understand God's love for us"*, or, *"I do not feel that God loves me."* I am not sure what more He could have done for us. As a matter of fact, He did everything for us already. All one has to do is first believe that Jesus suffered these horrible conditions to accomplish defeating death, in this case hell, so that we could enter heaven. The concept of love takes on a new construct for us. It is actually indescribable. Our Lord's heroic action is something He wants us to take advantage of for our own sakes.

All we have to do is believe first in Jesus. We need to consciously believe He came to save us through all He did to teach, show example, and endure until the end. It is in that moment that one has an innate spiritual desire to become more united to the Holy Trinity. The desire becomes an inexpressible need to fulfill. The author recommends that one says the Stations of the Cross on Fridays as part of a prayer routine. Even a short version of the stations will keep one growing in view of all that Jesus persevered through. The Stations are a prayer that intentionally recount and reflect on the high points in Jesus's Way to the Cross on Calvary. It comes with much grace each time one prays it.

Do you think that after contemplating all these actions our Lord completed for our sakes that this may bring the reader to a higher desire to serve Him? Do you think reflection on these actions can bring one to love God at a higher level? This is why Catholics still venerate a Crucifix versus an empty cross. Our Protestant brothers and sisters do not want to recognize that God still suffers. They unfortunately want to point only at His resurrection while forgetting the pain of the Holy Crucifixion. Many of our brothers and sisters suffer each day, and Christ still suffers with them. The Crucifix is a true reminder that suffering in the world still exists. The Crucifix signifies that God still suffers.

God still suffers mainly because there are large amounts of sin in the world. He is wounded continually by the many mortal sins that are committed. A crucifix is very relevant today. Thus, we pray for the conversions of sinners and "*offer up*" our struggles, sacrifices and sufferings to Him. We offer Him our acts of endurance, perseverance and strength.

The reason why the Catholic perspective is correct over just an empty cross is that there is no joy of the resurrection without the suffering of the crucifixion on the cross. Recall that Jesus's glory is in the cross. He reveals His Glory by demonstrating that He accepted the Cross and did not shy away, but bore our shame. We are the ones who deserved the shame but He shielded us from the embarrassment.

He still suffers for our world. Remember to unite your prayers of Thanksgiving for all the Lord has done and your prayers become all the more powerful and united to Heaven. Alleviate the Lord's sorrowful heart by doing your best to avoid all occasions of sin. Make that sacrifice as discussed in earlier chapters as a reparation for your sin and the sin of others. If you can clean your soul by going to confession, then do so immediately. If you are not Catholic you can make the following prayer a common practice. *"Oh my God, I am heartily sorry for having offended you. And I detest all of my sins because of your just punishment, but most of all because I have offended you my God who are all good and deserving of my love. I firmly resolve, with the help of Jesus, to sin no more and to avoid the near occasion of sin. Amen"*

CHAPTER TEN

For Those Suffering Anxiety, Despair, and Depression

For my brothers and sisters suffering daily anxiety, despair and depression

It is truly important that we reach out to those suffering from anxiety, or a dark despair, and unrelenting depression. If you are one of these suffering souls, this chapter is dedicated directly to you and is written for your benefit. The main thing you need to understand is that you have the ability to break these evil attempts at destroying your joy. You can break the thoughts that come to you that life is not worth living anymore, and that overall pain and feeling that you cannot pull yourself out from the lowest of places. I am going to explain how Jesus is far above these thoughts. He is the key to breaking out of this sheer misery, self-doubt, and terrible pain and sadness.

I was one of these people who suffered these debilitating scourges. I have a long lineage of people in my family who suffer this type of mental anguish and illness in my family history. It is known by exorcists and priests that past familial sins can be passed on to extending generations. Sometimes the origins are discovered, and sometimes they go unknown but can still be broken. I have had these chains snapped and torn. I give all the credit to our Lord and the motivation and cooperativeness He provided for my intellect to say "Yes!" to Him to being healed.

Cooperate with our Lord

Yes, one needs to cooperate and to believe and trust in Jesus's instruction to overcome the evil. This does not mean that I do not get melancholy and down from time to time. However, I have learned to give the glory to the Holy Trinity and in so doing, become stronger by speaking this language of heaven. It is most powerful to speak out praise and to give honor to our God. In so doing we vanquish these spirits because they simply cannot be around anything that gives homage, honor and thanksgiving to our Creator God. It helps to read the book of Psalms and Proverbs in scripture and very much hone in on the language that these books teach us. By recognizing vocally and without any shame that our God is all powerful becomes our foundation. Begging Him to provide for us His Mercy and to be covered with His precious blood routs and overpowers any spirit that tries to afflict us with worry, or that speaks hopelessness. Jesus's mighty sovereignty casts out the desolation that depression brings.

Evil hates gratitude towards God

Let us look at an example of how one should start the day. I suggest starting out very small and thank God for one or two things when you wake up and start saying your prayers. Grab your Holy Bible and turn to Psalms and start reading some of the language that the author, King David and others use to praise God. Here is an example: Psalm 18, "*I love you O Lord, my strength. The Lord is my rock, my fortress, and my deliverer, my God, my rock in whom I take refuge, my shield, and the horn of my salvation, my stronghold. I call upon the Lord, who is worthy to be praised; so I shall be saved from my enemies*". After reading a psalm such as this, break into your own praise and thank God with your entire mind and heart. This takes some effort and focus at times, but when you do it with happiness, this turns to joy. Pretty soon you are finding additional grace everywhere you look. I speak this again with truth as I have lived the life of anxiety and depression and I will not go back. Why? Because I have discovered that praising God and speaking the language of heaven has a power over spirits of affliction.

We alluded to this in prior chapters, but this is some specific instruction for those who need to be bolstered and given heart this very day! Get in the habit of praising God and thanking Him for the little things. This will allow you to magnify your thanksgiving and you will be that much more thankful and subsequently close to Him in larger things. Giving Him the praise and honor tells God you are serious about being His son or daughter. The day this hits you and you realize you belong to Him will be a day of great tears of joy, blessing, and immense consolation.

The seriousness of familial ties to sin and breaking these ties

Sometimes evil attaches to us through our family tree. Other times we inadvertently allow this evil to attach to us through spirits of affliction based on what we have chosen. Sometimes our past mistakes allow for evil to attach itself in spirits of affliction that cause us mental and physical harm not to mention the spiritual damage. This comes from choosing things other than God. Anger, pride, comparison to others, envy, jealously, lust, greed and being lazy and all the other major sins are actions that lead us away from God because He is none of these things. In finding your purpose, you discover and make conscious efforts to avoid these sins.

Here is where the Catholic faith has one up on every other religion. It is a serious game changer. When one recognizes these sins, or that your family lineage might have had these generational sins, it is time to go to confession, (I do not mean maybe). One good and honest confession is more powerful than exorcisms we are taught by the exorcists themselves.

After this confession you will find a desire to thank and praise Him outright, and you will find yourself praising Him in front of others because you want them to experience the same overjoyed realization you are now living. For those of you who are not Catholic, it is a path you can start down fairly easily at a local parish. Entering the Church as a full-fledged member will allow you to be able to receive confession. It is well worth the investment of time and prayers, and Jesus will help you get there. Many Catholics are willing to be sponsors and will attend the instructional with you as your support.

Eucharistic Adoration is our great gift

I am pleading with those of you who are so desolate or so nervous beyond relaxation to go spend time in Eucharistic Adoration. Even for those of you who are not Catholic, you can go to a Eucharistic Adoration Chapel and sit there in front of our Lord in the monstrance (the golden structure that holds the Eucharistic). Yes, He is truly present there in the chapel in that eucharistic host. He will surely reveal His presence to you. All you have to do is sit there in silence and speak to Him in your heart and listen for His response. When you are in His presence, then beg for all the graces that He wants to bestow down upon you. Then be open to what you feel.

It might not happen then and there, but within the next few days, you will notice the correlation and discover that He has heard your prayers and petitions. Our God wants to heal, and remember, His Mercy is His greatest attribute. He wants to remove your sins, but you need to cooperate and be sorrowful and accept forgiveness. This will start to break the stronghold the spirits of affliction have on you. It is only a matter of time before Jesus has completely healed you.

Finally, for those of you suffering so badly that you are considering taking your own life, you first need to seek professional help. It is not weak to ask for help. Reach out to a professional who can help and who understands what you are experiencing. There is no shame in this!

Until you can get in front of that professional person, however, we can stop and say, "Jesus, I surrender to you, please help me!" It is not magic or a spiritual control tool, but by surrendering to Jesus it is one of the most powerful spiritual states that one can enter into. It means that you turn all worry, fear, and hurt over to Him at that moment. One can start to expect a miracle and that Jesus will take care of it, all of it. Again, we reference the (Surrender Novena) in Appendix A for this prayer of trust. It will transform your faith and leave no room for any doubt that your King and Savior, wants you to be healed. There are many faith-filled professionals that will walk this recovery path with you.

Turn to our Lord when you are suffering and start down the path of healing and repair. It is what He does. It is the power of Jesus. It is what He wants to do for us. There is no evil spirit that can withstand His power. He will free you. He loves you. Absorb that love and look for ways to thank and praise Him. Little by little your life will be changed by the Holy Providence of God.

Prayer: *"I praise you Jesus, Almighty Merciful and Awesome King. Thank you for your wonderful love and saving me from all evil. I honor your Kingship and am so grateful for your great comfort and Holiness! Please show me how to become closer to you, and to love you back with all my heart, mind, and soul. I love you Jesus! Jesus, I Trust in You! Mary, Most Holy Mother of Jesus, Queen of the Angels, show us how to honor your Son, as You do! My beloved guardian angel, please tell God the Father, thank you this day for creating me and freeing me from sin. Help me to choose God in all my decisions as you do O beloved guardian. O Holy Spirit, help me to do what you are asking of me to do!"*

CHAPTER ELEVEN

The Mission Within Our Purpose

Get to the point where you can start to fulfill the mission

Ok, so we have established and concluded that our main goal, our purpose is to get to heaven. We are well on our way to knowing, loving, and serving God through our virtuous living. We are following the example of Jesus to the Father. We are observing all of God's laws and trying to live the Good News of Jesus. This is when we need to consider one more important factor.

We stated we need to honor God by doing His Will. We learned that Jesus is the Way to the Father. We found out that Jesus lived His whole reality on being focused on doing the will of God. We also discovered that no one can come to the Father except through Jesus. We determined that virtuous living is good, and that we can offer this to God like Jesus did. We ascertained that Jesus is Love and Mercy and Truth. In all of these premises, we then conclude that we need to do then what Jesus asks of us to be worthy of our dwelling place and to demonstrate our love for God.

While we are working on honing these virtues and striving for our heavenly abode, we come to realize that Jesus gives us a mission within our purpose of getting to paradise. Yes. We are followers of Jesus and believe in Him and confess that He is our Lord. We need to take seriously all He has instructed and commanded. He gives us a command before He ascended into heaven after His Resurrection. We are to do a combination of things that He gave us for final instructions as His disciples.

In the Gospel of Mark, Jesus's departing words are these: *"'Go into all the world and proclaim the good news to the whole creation. The one who believes and is baptized will be saved; but the one who does not believe will be condemned"* (Mark 16 : 15-16). Here we are charged with the order to tell everyone about Jesus and all that He represents and has done. Well, if we are finding our purpose and on the way to heaven, this is being displayed in the way we live our lives and the way we honor God. The more direct answer is proactively going out and introducing others to Jesus by what you know of Him. This is both exciting and challenging because we know that there is a great reward for us and others and we want them to know what we know. However, as in our own struggles, the evil one will do what he can to make us feel awkward, unworthy, and he will plant seeds of doubt in our ability to convey the good news. This is where we ask Jesus to help us be bold, daring, and reach out to others on His account! This is where your strength and courage virtues come back into play.

The second part of the instructions from our Lord as He rises to the clouds is slightly more direct. In Matthew's Gospel, Jesus declares, *"'All authority in heaven and on earth has been given to me. Go therefore and make disciples of all nations, baptizing them in the name of the Father, and of the Son, and of the Holy Spirit, and teaching them to obey everything that I have commanded you. And remember, I am with you always, to the end of the age.'"* (28:18-20). He wants us to engage those who do not yet know Him. We are to speak openly and with confidence regarding Jesus. This means we do not have to be embarrassed or hidden in speaking about Him. We are simply to help others know, love, and serve Him Jesus who will introduce them to the Father. We do all of this while we journey on our purpose. We fulfill this mission as we go along.

The life of the Christian is not always easy. We often offer much to God in our sufferings and sacrifices, but we do it with a joyful and peace filled spirit. In so doing, we live the life we are supposed to live and we find ourselves loving God more and more. We find ourselves wanting to do good things for Him and others. We uncover our true identity and strive for our treasure in heaven while loving our neighbor, our families and God. Thank you for fulfilling your mission within your purpose. See you in heaven!

CHAPTER TWELVE

Encouragement from Those Who Have Gone Before Us

Let us learn from others who have walked in front of us

Time to circle-back and meander again towards the purpose for this writing. Remember that this narrative is meant to help you understand some of the key concepts that rally us to persevere, endure and use our strength to get us through towards our dwelling in heaven. We use basic virtues to help us demonstrate love for God and others. In so doing, we become more cognizant that life contains a very meaningful purpose. We reviewed examples, chiefly that of our Lord, who perfectly demonstrated these virtues. It is important to appreciate that many good people have gone before us. It is important to personalize this and recognize that ordinary people like us struggled, suffered and sacrificed to get to their final destination as well. We can gain some encouragement to contemplate the examples of some and what they had to deal with in their own lives. Let us turn to the stories of some great saints and examples of extraordinary people who you might be able to relate to. In so doing, you may find a reinforcing encouragement or inspiration to deal with what you might be experiencing in your own life.

The following examples are meant to assist the reader in understanding that not too much under the sun has changed since the fall in the garden. Meaning man and woman still struggle with the same things as of old. People struggle in this life we determined because of original sin and the great conflict between good and evil. Remember that you are created good and that God wants you to be with Him forever. The idea and hope are that telling the following stories will perhaps assist the reader. Finding a correlation and evaluating the same struggles famously encountered by others is the goal by reading these accounts. One may determine that the same, or very similar problems that the saints had, the reader is now experiencing in their current lives. These stories are recalled so that one can marvel at the virtues these people demonstrated in making their own way to God on route to their dwelling place.

That is really the bottom line. To live our lives for God and ultimately obtain our heavenly dwelling with those we love. The author believes these stories to be some of the most heroic displays of virtue that people could exhibit. Their efforts to show good examples themselves, while dealing with toil and trouble, proved they loved and trusted God for His faithfulness. Each was true to both themselves and God. Let us reflect on a few of the following stories.

Clyde Arthur Russell, Role Model Extraordinaire

I have to write of a very just man, a man who respected God with humility, courage, and strength. A person who demonstrated endurance and perseverance through some of the most challenging times in history. My Grandfather on my mother's side was born Clyde Arthur Russell. He was of Scottish and German descent. He was a happy by nature man, one that cared deeply for his family and his country.

He had a very misfortunate childhood, one that involved much pain and loss. He grew as the oldest of three children to Irwin and Marta Russell in Anoka, Minnesota. He grew up in humble surroundings where his father contracted an illness and died when Clyde was six. Clyde had a younger sister, Margaret and a younger brother Glen who he loved much. Clyde tried to help support the family even at a young age. Clyde was destined to continue his course in life and God had His providence and blessing around him more than once in his life.

As an example, Clyde had two friends that he would go to the local excavation site where sand and gravel were mined to support the area in local construction materials. Each day they would venture to and play with their toys at the base of the large sand and gravel hills. He did this until his mother discovered what the boys were innocently doing each day to pass the time. When Clyde's mother learned of the potential danger of playing around a construction site, she forbade Clyde to go with his friends explaining that he could be in eminent danger. Despite Clyde's disappointment at not being able to go, he obeyed his mother. He understood the value of the virtue of obedience. That same day, both friends, after trying to get Clyde to attend with them, both tragically died as they were buried at the base of a large sand and gravel hill. The hill let loose from the recent rains and Marta's instinct had saved her son from an untimely death. Clyde lived through this as he had much to achieve yet in life.

Tragedy struck the family again as the Russell children lost their mother to cancer when Clyde was age 13. The family had to be split up and Clyde lost the ability to see his sister and brother. He lived with his maternal Grandfather, a blacksmith who had Clyde help and assist to help the family pay for his brother and sister who went to live with other relatives. Clyde did all kinds of jobs and was reunited for a brief time with his little brother. Clyde tried to support the two of them by joining a traveling entertainment group circus where his talents allowed him to earn an income to survive and keep living. His Grandfather passed away in the meantime leaving Clyde and his brother and sister true orphans.

As time when on and Clyde learned other trades. He worked many hours of construction and somehow survived the Great Depression. He and his friends at a very young age decided in 1939 to join the local gun club to learn to shoot and participate in sport shooting at the Marine corps Reserves Gun Club. Not long after joining, Clyde was drafted into the Marine Corp during World War II. He served in the first major amphibious force assault battle of the Pacific Theater at Tulagi and the last major battle of the Pacific at Okinawa, Japan. Back in Anoka, he had been dating Mary Alice Stack my grandmother and the two of them became married during one of his Pacific military leaves. Clyde was deployed while his first daughter Carol was born, and endured this heartache of being away from his young family. He was deployed two other separate times back to the Pacific and also had a second daughter Rosella during this time.

While serving in the Pacific, Clyde was wounded seriously in the battle of Guadalcanal where the Americans experienced 80% casualties. Clyde crawled under a destroyed piece of amphibious armor after being seriously hit with shrapnel and losing profuse amounts of blood where he was able to stop some of the bleeding and maintain his life. He recalled having a presence around him that he said had to be God's angel protecting him. Clyde saw much horror in the battles of the Pacific and lost many friends he stated. While he earned two purple hearts for his valor, he was bitter to his dying day that war had taken so much from him. Clyde however persevered and went on to have eight children and twenty-six grandchildren. Clyde was a construction superintendent after the war and was someone who went on to do good things for society including co-patenting two major electronic features used in the auto industry.

Clyde had the chance to reunite after the war with his sister and brother who had grown and now had families of their own. Clyde's endurance, perseverance and strength were and are an example of heroic continuation of life when moments he encountered proved were times when he could have given up, when he might have not gone on. Clyde went on to convert to Catholicism at the end of his life.

Clyde had many years of nightmares of all he endured during his six-year military service period. He also acquired Parkinson's disease the last ten years of his life, and finally prostate cancer. He patiently and courageously did not give up during this time of physical incapacity and demonstrated remarkable character as he lived life until he was 84. Clyde Russell was just one example of exemplary endurance, perseverance, and strength that this author hopes will somehow encourage readers who learn of his "never give up" attitude. Clyde had a deep respect and humility at the grandeur of God. He never was brought up with religion, but accepted the Catholic Religion as the true Church. He attended mass often and was a great example of a convert to the faith.

Clyde was a just man and taught his grandchildren the meaning of being just and humble in this world. I will be forever in his debt. His favorite saying was, "It was just when I began to realize that I was a fool in this world that I truly began to know something"! Thank you to both Clyde and Mary for being part of the greatest American generation ever! Those who saved the world at the time. Those who showed us the meaning of perseverance and endurance while loving each other and their family.

Saint Thomas More, Model of Perseverance

In showcasing particular people's stories to use as illustrations for these virtues, I am hoping to provide both a way for the reader to connect to the situations regarding the individual's circumstances, conditions, and instances they live through. The intent is for the reader to find inspiration and encouragement in all of the hardships and blessings that are modeled by these cases in point. When considering the lives of the Saints, all of these people lived extraordinary lives in their commitment to the God the Father, God the Son, and the Holy Spirit. All in accordance to the teachings and magisterium of the Holy Catholic Church. In contemplating these vast numbers of examples in the Holy Church, certain Saints come to mind for their exemplary demonstration of how they lived out these three virtues. One of the Saints that come to mind is St. Thomas More.

The author here is not able to give St. Thomas More's life and history justice in this brief paradigm, however, there is a book if the reader wishes to learn more called a "Portrait of Courage", by Gerard Wegemer. This is an outstanding semi-biography of St. Thomas's life and it does a great job in prefacing the times and all that the saint went through in successfully defending the Holy Sacrament of Marriage and ultimately Jesus Christ's bride the Holy Catholic Church. St. Thomas More used his great intellectual and social skill gifts, but was unrighteously disciplined for being the best representative in England for the Catholic Church at the time. For history's sake, in England, the Church was true to Rome until King Henry the VIII deviated drastically from the Pope's and Church's authority. He ultimately pronounced himself the Pope of his own version of the Church which became the Anglican Church we know today. This is why the Anglican Church has much in common with the Roman Catholic Church of today. This needs to be prefaced in order to understand what was at stake for Sir Thomas More, otherwise known as Thomas More, or St. Thomas More.

St. Thomas More (along with Bishop John Fischer his counterpart in England in the late fourteen and early fifteen hundreds) were high ranking officials in the English government in the fourteen and fifteen hundreds. Columbus had recently discovered America. Much controversy was happening in Europe in general. He and St. Bishop Fischer were ultimately forced to make the decision to obey God or obey a mortal man that wielded power. As is always, there was a fierce battle between good and evil. They were both asked to stand by God's Holy Church and Hierarchy, and or give in to something they interiorly knew was betraying Jesus Christ and His laws set forth by the Holy Catholic Church. The topic in consideration was in regards to the sacrament of Holy Matrimony to be exact. Both men had to decide whether it was going to cost them their lives, or more conveniently give in to a ruthless crazed power-hungry king, one who wanted to selfishly make himself the Pope at the time and rewrite the rules to fit his sinful lifestyle. King

Henry had already been married legitimately once in the Church, but wanted to divorce his wife and marry another. This was not, in the eyes of the Church going to be a valid marriage as the King had already consummated and was married to Queen Catherine of Aragon.

Born in 1477, Thomas More was born of respectable parents in England that came from the bakery, brewing and law backgrounds. Thomas was attending college when Columbus discovered the New World to the West, and was intrigued by the discovery, but was destined to govern and guide England at a time when the Protestant revolution and Martin Luther were breaking away and causing great upheaval during the early to mid-fifteen hundreds. Thomas debated Luther and wrote many "dialogues" against what Luther was unconvincingly trying to argue regarding free will and other heresy of the time. Luther was reluctant to debate Thomas More because of his brilliance and also because of his pride which resulted in one of the largest errors of history, that of breaking with the Catholic Church and leading millions astray.

Thomas worked his way up through English government where he held positions such as undersheriff, Parliament's Financial Secretary, Speaker of the House of Commons, was a lawyer for the powerful Merchants guild in London, Sheriff of London, and finally he was Chancellor of England as he worked his way to the 2nd highest in command in England, 2nd only to King Henry the VIII.

As it ironically turned out, Thomas and King Henry the VIII grew up together and were like best friends as children, teenagers and as young adults. Thomas was a brilliant poet, and had a love of philosophy. He studied law and was held in esteem by most of London and by many in other countries and universities he visited. He was married twice, his first wife Jane Colt passed away after their sixth year of marriage after having three daughters and a son. Thomas was perplexed as he was grieved about what to do with four small children. He married within thirty-days after Jane's passing. Many women were interested in Thomas because of his notoriety as a great lawyer, but he was also a very kind and likeable man. Alice Middleton was his second wife and together they had eight children in total including Alice's daughter from a previous marriage and two adopted daughters. Thomas lived to have many grandchildren as well. Thomas always attended Holy Days and Sunday obligations and made it a point to teach his children the faith. St. Thomas More was known for his wit, humor, brilliant thinking, and even being a literary author at the time.

St. Thomas served the King for many years and as mentioned before often stopped by to talk to the young prince Henry and introduce a new friend. At one-point, young prince Henry had "strong beliefs and substantial piety", (Wegemer, pg. 128). As time grew on and as St. Thomas More served the King as Lord Chancellor, Ann Boleyn became King Henry's mistress as he was already married to Queen Catherine, and to make the situation more complicated, Catherine had been married to Henry's brother Arthur. King Henry used an excuse to divorce Catherine citing the book of Leviticus 20:21 which stated if a man shall take his brother's wife, it is an impurity; he has uncovered his brother's nakedness; they shall be childless." So, Henry, while having a mistress of his own after approximately seven years of knowing Ann Boleyn, used this excuse to divorce his wife Catherine to marry Anne Boleyn. Now Henry and Catherine did have a daughter, Mary, who was eleven at the time of Henry's claim. The truth was that Catherine and Arthur had never consummated their marriage because of Arthur's health.

The reason for these details is to set the stage as those closest to the King, including the clergy and Church officials, all knew these details. This put St. Thomas More in a very peculiar position. It was such a high-level scandal that this take place for the King to divorce the Queen, since the marriage between Henry and Catherine was viewed as valid by the Church.

Now all close to the King were expected to concede their faith and "go along to get along" with the King. However, other officials were not originally approving of the proposed actions. Catherine tried for seven years to fight the divorce and expected high ranking officials such as the Pope, her nephew Emperor Charles V, who was the Holy Roman Emperor, and also the King of Spain and other bishops to come to her aid, but none of these had enough courage except St. Thomas More and Bishop John Fischer.

Eventually, St. Thomas More was called upon by the King to support his decision to divorce Catherine. St. Thomas had seen this coming for years, and as the King finally drew closer to completing his action he called upon St. Thomas More to advocate and give his approval to the unlawful decision. St. Thomas More had the esteem of the people and many people wanted to know what he was going to do. St. Thomas knew he was in the spotlight. St. Thomas actually stepped down ahead of time from the position of being Lord Chancellor as he saw the writing on the wall.

In the meantime, there was many secular pressures coming on King Henry to steer him away from his faith. Henry was becoming more determined not to let the cleric's influence him or England as there was already an underlying power struggle between the Church and Henry's State. The reason Henry appointed Thomas to the position of Lord Chancellor was that he did not want a Cardinal or Bishop to have that much influence again on his Kingship. Nevertheless, Thomas resigned in 1532 after having served from 1529. He did this as to avoid having to continually be in the service of the King as he knew the divorce was coming. He also could see that King Henry was going to make himself a Pope as Henry had many and frequent arguments with the current clergy and members of Parliament that were faithful to the Church. The other issue was that Henry believed he was right and possessed a vindictive personality.

All this was occurring while Thomas was doing his best to serve England, his family, and the Lord by doing what he could. As Chief Justice, Thomas heard on average about one thousand cases per year.

This was double the workload what the previous Lord Chancellor, Cardinal Wolsey, had done on average, and the people considered his predecessor a remarkable chief justice before Thomas. This speaks to Thomas's work ethic and endurance as he cared for the people in England. He worked diligently to keep the country on the right path all the while he knew his reckoning was coming. In thinking about the stress that Thomas must have undertaken to begin preparing his family for possibly the worse must have taken its toll both physically and mentally. Thomas's wife was upset with Thomas for resigning as she was interested in keeping the family's popularity and status at a high level, but Thomas tried to reason with her to understand that he had to serve God first. This brought some strife in the marriage, but Thomas's keen wit and humor was what he used to keep things together.

As Henry became more obsessed with becoming an Emperor of England for the sake of ruling both Church and State, it was fueled by and anger increased by "offended pride" (Wegemer, pg. 143). Even after Thomas resigned, he tried diligently to reach the King's conscience. Thomas stayed in the good graces of the King and called the King his friend even after a harsh scrutiny a year later. Things changed however in 1534 when it was stated that the King wanted Thomas dead and requested Thomas's indictment. (Wegemer, pg. 149). King Henry wanted Thomas to concede and agree with him about becoming Emperor and to marry Ann Boleyn. Thomas prayed and thought of all the great saints who went before him for fifteen hundred years and the sacrifices they had to make. What great strength and perseverance Thomas had to show to both his family and those friends watching. His daughters, out of fear, were somewhat trying to make him also concede so that nothing bad would happen to their father.

Thomas displaying virtue, silence, and relying on his good reputation continued the good fight until he was imprisoned. The Arch Bishop of the time folded and granted an "annulment" to the King for his marriage to Catherine. A short time later the King went ahead and married and coronated Ann Boleyn as the new Queen. Thomas refused to go to this coronation. In July of 1533, as Wegemer describes, Pope Clement the VII condemned Henry's divorce despite the Arch Bishop's approval of an annulment. As time went on the King was calling for the House of Lord's to indict Thomas for treason on trumped-up charges for his support of the Pope at the time and his non-approval of the King's new wife. In April of 1534, Thomas was imprisoned in the Tower of London, until July 5th of 1535. For almost 16 months where his health failed, and loneliness and misery were much, Thomas persevered and endured.

Thomas had to try and console his family for his impending death, and still tried hard to convince members of the King's cabinet that there was no reason for imprisonment, yet these evildoers continued to intimidate and plan a strategy for killing Thomas for his public opposition to the King. The reader has to understand that there were many others who opposed King Henry's decisions to go against the Church and these were monks, priests, and faithful people to true Holy Church. Often times these people would be marched in front of Thomas's window on their way to be hanged, drawn, and quartered for punishment in not obeying the King. Can you imagine the interior torture that Thomas endured and that of his family?

Again, the author cannot give a fully proper perspective and appreciation for all that was happening that Thomas persevered through. On July 1st of 1535, Thomas sustained a trial of "spectacular injustice" (Wegemer, pg. 218). This trial was so corrupt with falsehoods that even the commoners understood that the verdict was extreme absurdity. On July 6th of 1535 the evil one's influence on Henry brought about the ultimate betrayal, and Thomas's suffering on this earth ended as he went to the guillotine. He was joyful even upon death as he made jokes to the executioner. St. Thomas More is the epitome of what good people sometimes brave in this life to fulfill God's Holy and yet perfect will. He demonstrated that those who may be in power over worldly affairs can often take advantage of others, but Thomas demonstrated sacrifice and deep love to Jesus and His Holy Church. Thomas More is the patron saint of civil servants and politicians to name a few. Thank you, St. Thomas More for your exemplary example of virtue.

God always brings good out of evil, and St. Thomas More has been a beacon to many people throughout history involved with injustices. There is even the St. Thomas More Society in America who defends religious freedom and those who are being unjustly accused or represented. St. Thomas More can give us all encouragement to face the betrayals and deceptions to fight false charges, to not give in to the enticement of evil and power bullying even unto death. St. Thomas More please pray for us and help us to not be afraid of confronting the evil one in his many forms. St. Thomas More followed in the footsteps of Christ and suffered injustice. We pray that we will be able to follow Christ more closely despite what we have to live through. Thank you, St. Thomas for your stellar strength, perseverance, and endurance.

Saint Sr. Faustina Kowalska (The Divine Mercy Saint)

On the theme of people whose persistence countered this world's many crosses, is another Catholic saint whose life and mission I would like to underscore. That of St. Sr. Faustina Kowalska. Why are we focused on the lives of some saints?

The Catholic Church goes through a rigorous process to evaluate, critique, and scrutinize the lives of anyone who ultimately is named a saint by the Holy Church. This means that to have the title saint conferred upon your name means that the Church can say with certainty that this person is among the elect of heaven. In other-words, the person who has this designation given to them has had their life reviewed and their deeds, and accomplishments towards serving God indeed found worthy to believe. Thus, this term is bestowed upon them. This means they have lived lives of extraordinary virtue, such as faith, love, hope and those virtues we are considering in this writing. They are in heaven. We can access them to help us by asking them to intercede for us. They are more than happy to help us as long as we are in a state of grace and looking to ultimately serve God and become a saint ourselves.

With this in mind, Faustina Kowalska was a humble Polish girl whose life was astonishingly amazing in many respects. She was one who would suffer everything for Christ and suffer she did. Faustina would exemplify what it meant to endure, be perseverant, and to be strong in many adversities. Hers was a soul so loved by Jesus, that he told her that she was the one chosen to help prepare the world for His Second Coming! Yes! How would you like to be that favored a soul, that blessed, and have that much weight put on your shoulders all at the same time? Faustina was up for the challenge, because she learned to rely solely on Jesus.

Faustina became Saint Sister Faustina Kowlalska. So important was she and her mission to the Church, that Pope John Paul II named her the first saint of the new millennium in the year 2000. St. Faustina was the secretary of God's finest attribute, God's unfathomable Divine Mercy!

Faustina was born into a very poor polish family. Was the third daughter in a family of ten children. Her first name was Helen and she was given many strange graces as a child that went into her teen age years. She was often ridiculed because she knew she wanted to enter the convent and her parents were against that because they were both poor and could not afford a dowry and because they loved and favored her. Helen had a very keen wit and was also a very funny person. She attracted many children because of her story telling talents. She was also very skilled at handling the family dairy cattle and could lead them to pasture without fencing and without the cows wandering into shared fields with plenty of crops. This was something that marveled many. (Mercy My Mission, Sr. Sophia Michalenko)

Helen worked many jobs as a house maid and traveled to many towns in Poland doing various types of work. Her prayer life grew and she was often unable to sleep due to seeing "a strange light" when she tried to sleep (Mercy My Mission, Sr. Sophia Michalenko). She struggled with one of the spiritual phases that saints and those growing closer to God often experience in the "dark night of the soul". Helen felt she was called to be religious, but continued to work and also to try to distract herself and focus on going out with her sisters. She tried to become more worldly with finer clothes and sophisticated things. She often went to dances, but she was still unfulfilled and unhappy.

One night at a dance, it is said that Helen was in a torment. She was not enjoying her time that evening. Then, in the dancehall, she encountered an inexplicable great mystical experience. Jesus said to her, *"How long shall I put up with you and how long will you keep putting me off?"* Helen left the dance and went to a nearby Church. She then asked God what His will for her was. He said to her, '*Go at once to Warsaw, you will enter a convent there.*" (Michalenko, pg. 11). It was there that Helen, though very sad at the idea that she was going to hurt her parents, decided to obey God and the feeling she had since she was seven.

Again, I cannot give satisfactory detail in these contexts to describe all that Helen was going to have to endure. She was to be the one chosen and holy enough to provide the world with Jesus in the Divine Mercy. Helen suffered much at the convent. She suffered and sacrificed also at the convents that she was transferred back and forth to. She had superiors who were unsympathetic. Most did not understand her calling. She had difficulty relaying events to her confessor and spiritual advisor priests. Her fellow sisters did not know of her interior piety, nor the promises she made to Jesus. She had promised Jesus to be inwardly close to Him and suffer for Him without any evidence shown or known by others regarding her private spiritual life. Many of her fellow sisters treated her with contempt. Yet, Faustina showed these same sister religious nothing but respect, love, and incredible humility.

She persevered and it required years before she could profess her final vows and become a full-fledged religious.

All the while her life progressed, Faustina was in conversation with our Lord. She was learning experiencing His Divine Mercy. Divine Mercy is something that everyone needs to study to learn the depths of our Lord's remarkable essence. The book this author suggests reading is a biography of Sister Kowalska by Sister Sophia Michalenko. It took years for our Lord to teach Faustina the great details and aspects of His Divine Mercy, what it meant for the world, and how it was to be utilized before his Second Coming.

Jesus once told Faustina (the name she took upon taking her vows), *"Tell all people, my daughter, that I am Love and Mercy itself. When a soul approaches Me with trust, I fill it with such an abundance of graces that it cannot contain them within itself, but radiates them to other souls"* (Michalenko, pg. 155), and that, *"Before I come as a just Judge, I first open wide the door of My mercy. He who refuses to pass through the door of My mercy must pass through the door of My justice…"* (Michalenko, pg. 160). OUCH! Who hears our Lord say these words of warning and does not have chills run down their spine or have a mini-panic attack? Our Lord pleads with us to utilize his Mercy, and to obtain as many graces as one can. This was Faustina's mission to deliver this message to the world. She had to suffer much however, in her adult life to obtain the conversion of many souls.

Faustina underwent much physically as she grew older. She maintained harsh personal penances and offered many things as sacrifices to save souls. Her efforts kept her country Poland from being destroyed because of the sin that was occurring at this time (abortion), right before World War II. For those who do not understand the concept of a penance, it is mystical in nature, and is typically a self-mortification of sorts and or a devotion or set of prayers said to God to "offset' or "repair" the harms that sin does to our souls. Done correctly, and with a holy intention, are very favored by heaven. Here, one undertakes and does something that one would not typically or rather do normally. It is done in order to be "offered up", or to compensate for oneself or another's sins that have offended and hurt God who is all good. Fasting, as discussed earlier is a form of doing a penance as well as it is a disciplined action one makes for God.

Faustina offered remarkable penances during her life. These penances accompanied by sacrifices make an atonement for our own sins or the sins of others when offered to God. These are required to be done in a state of grace (no mortal sin on our own souls). Sacrifice is different than a penance. It often involves a loss of, or giving up something, or renouncing something that one would commonly like to enjoy or have. One again offers it to God to atone for some sinfulness one has committed. To sacrifice and offer penance according to Catholics is honorable, and necessary for our own souls. We either do this here on earth while we live or we take it on in Purgatory after this life. Nevertheless, one must atone for sins committed and their temporal effects on our souls either during our earthly lives or in Purgatory.

This commentary is provided here because Faustina's work included bringing to the forefront once again, the spiritual necessity of these actions. There are more detailed explanations that other authors can provide, however, suffice it to mention that these definitions will help you understand the context of Faustina and other saint's motives and actions.

This is not to be confused with having one's sins forgiven by Jesus. As this happens when we have a contrite heart and seek absolution in the confessional. This is referred to as the Sacrament of Reconciliation and or the Sacrament of Penance. (Please do not confuse the noun and verbs of the term penance).

Faustina suffered the grueling pains of having Tuberculosis. Anyone who knows this disease understands that back in the 1920's and 1930's, before they found antibiotics that could help cure the disease, it was a slow and painful death. It typically landed one in a sanitorium, or place of recovery with other Tuberculosis patients. This happened to Faustina.

Faustina endured this disease and persevered in serving the Lord with much anguish and torment. Faustina would take on great sufferings, but would be rewarded with the graces and knowledge to all the secrets of the Divine Mercy, which she chronicled in her diary. This is where the world gets most of its knowledge that our Lord provided regarding His greatest quality.

Faustina would go on to complete many atonements for her own convent, for abortions throughout Poland and for the doctors who performed these abortions. When describing the pains she endured for the atonement of these mothers who allowed the killing of their children, she stated, *"At eight o'clock I was seized with such violent pains that I had to go to bed at once. I was convulsed with pain for three hours, that is, until eleven o'clock at night. No medicine had an effect on me, and whatever I swallowed I threw up. At times, the pain caused me to lose consciousness. Jesus helped me realize that in this way I took part in His Agony in the Garden, and that He himself allowed these sufferings in order to offer reparation to God for the souls murdered in the wombs of wicked mothers. I have gone through these sufferings three times now.......the following day I feel very weak."* (Michalenko, pg. 171).

Faustina loved the Lord immensely and begged Him to take her to heaven. The Lord asked Faustina to suffer much. He had a spectacular plan for her although He allowed for her to suffer and partake in his passion and agony.

Faustina also had the privilege of bearing the wounds of Christ. That meant she had the nail hole wounds in both feet and hands and the piercing in the side that Christ suffered. He allowed her to experience these in the utmost and extreme intensity as these brought great graces to humanity. Those graces are ones we are receiving now in the first 25 years of the 21st century.

Sr. Faustina tried her best to work and live a contemplative life during her years in the convent. She was sent to various convents for different tasks over the course of her sisterhood. She finally had to be sent to a sanitarium, a hospital just for those suffering from tuberculosis. This is where she finally succumbed to the disease. Not before however, Christ completed in her all the graces, the Divine Mercy promises, the Divine Mercy picture, and all the entries of what Christ wanted her to share regarding this "unfathomable Mercy". Can you relate at all to having endured and persevered as Faustina did in order to serve God and accomplish great things for His kingdom? More people do not give themselves credit for trying to do the will of God despite many hardships. Hopefully people learn to lean on God during these exasperating and radical times when people are tested to the limit. May God be the source of your strength in trying to persevere through all trials.

When thinking of Faustina and other saint's lives, I think of the very popular Christian song that has captured many Catholic and Christian audiences in both worship services and as inspirational music. The second verse to the song "*In Christ Alone*" by Keith Getty and Stuart Townsend, the lyrics especially point out that we need to recognize that Jesus took on everything for us and gives us his Mercy to alleviate our sins, and appease God's justice. Faustina helped bring to us this understanding even more so, and she lived and did what she could to save other souls. So, we ponder, *"In Christ alone, who took on flesh, Fullness of God in helpless babe. This gift of love and righteousness, scorned by the ones He came to save. 'Til on that cross, as Jesus died, the wrath of God was satisfied, for every sin, on Him was laid, here in the death of Christ I live, I live."*

Sophia, God's Faithful Servant

There are times in life when we think our plight is the worse than others. We think the cross we bear is worse than all others. Then we realize life can be cold, unloving, harsh, and tempt us to be without hope. These are the times we refocus focus on giving God thanks for our lives.

It is during some of these distressing situations when things appear bleak that one needs to look at the example of some of the most enduring yet joyful people in the world. When one considers the life of those with a disease such as cerebral palsy that often create physical, mental, and emotional limitations, usually from birth, it opens one's eyes and heart. A circumstance of helplessness that comes from the disease and the suffering that person endures can portray an impossible situation. If you look hard at that individual with heartfelt compassion, humility surfaces and then overcomes your senses. You are suddenly acutely aware of what some people have to endure for their entire lives.

When looking upon these individuals, it is not uncommon to first consider that it may be exceedingly difficult to experience joy and any satisfaction from life. Rather, struggle, pain, and extreme frustration in just trying to live a somewhat normal daily life is what one perceives.

When I consider the story of Sophia, I remain humble, somewhat ashamed of my selfishness, and become overall embarrassed regarding the way I have lived life at times. Much unlike how Sophia has lived hers. When we feel like we are at our end, and cannot come up with enough strength to persevere and endure what life is dealing out to us at the moment, it is then that we must consider the remarkable and heroic examples that come from some in our communities that carry this cross.

Sophia was the first born of a young couple in the 1980's. Mary, Sophia's mother, was a happy person by nature and a very loving and caring mother. Sophia's father, Robert, was a young parent that was overwhelmed when faced with the reality that his new born daughter would forever struggle with the effects from cerebral palsy. He could not deal with his daughter's reality and the struggles that Sophia would encounter her entire life. He was not able to cope with his responsibilities in raising a daughter with disabilities. Robert left the marriage and abandoned the family due to the circumstances.

Mary was not only embarrassed of the situation, but devastated by Robert's desertion. Her family was incredibly supportive and did their best to assist Mary raise Sophia as a single mother. Sophia was responsive to hugs, loving gestures, and was very affectionate towards her two aunts, Susan and Anna, and to her grandparents Helen and John.

Other members of the family, while very saddened by Mary's situation, did not know how to helpfully respond in caring for Sophia's many physical needs. They did not know how to support Mary in this type of direct care situation. Nevertheless, Sophia exhibited joy and was always smiling in her wheel chair. Mary also demonstrated strength and tried to keep positive.

Sophia's physical needs were much. She had difficulty breathing due to the mucous that her disease produced and would need to be cared for intently with suctioning measures. She could do nothing for herself and had to be physically restrained in the wheel chair to sit upright.

Mary heroically did her best and offered her child as much love and support as a mother could offer. As other family members interacted, our hearts broke when we looked upon Sophie. This nickname affectionately caught on, and she would smile back in approval.

God blessed Mary for her perseverance and what she was enduring. When Sophie was about five years old, Mary met Nicholas (Nick), a man who owned a company that would transport individuals with disabilities such as Sophie's. As would be the case, Nick and Mary developed a bonding relationship because of Sophie, and were married within approximately a year of their meeting. Things were looking up for Sophie's family.

Sophie continued to grow, and she was blessed with two brothers and two sisters that also helped care for and provide love to Sophie. As the years passed, Sophie's body grew and she became a beautiful young lady, while unable to truly communicate, she did her best to let others know her needs and what made her happy. She was very close to certain individuals, and showed the greatest love and determination to live life even though she needed round-the-clock care.

Sophie demonstrated the love of Christ in that she was always smiling and filled with joy. She was born on the Feast Day of St. Blaise, Bishop and Martyr, February 3rd. I shared this birthday with Sophie. I would think of her on my birthday and would wish her well. I was reminded at least once each year that Sophie was so very strong in her continued daily living despite her disease.

There were times when Sophia would experience sadness. Sophie eventually reached an age where entering a group home was a necessary step to support her care. While Sophie transitioned to group home living, Mary could continue to focus on the growing challenges of keeping Sophia healthy and the quality of Sophie's care. Mary was also able to maintain the rest of the family's needs. It was hard to have Sophie move out from Mary's direct motherly care.

While this transition was difficult, the family never stopped visiting Sophia. Sophia lost her mother Mary to a bout with cancer after a three-year struggle. Sophia also lost her step dad Nick to overriding health issues about one and a half years later. Sophia still sees her brothers and sisters occasionally as they have lives of their own, but Sophia continues to this day to live for Christ and offer Him a daily struggle with her cross of cerebral palsy.

When I think of all the pleasures of life that Sophia is unable to experience and enjoy, I also reflect on my own cross and how God gives each one of us our own particular sufferings to bear. (Remember, we share in our sufferings with Christ and He shares His love for us with granting us eternal life). I think of how strong Sophie is and how great her life will be in heaven as she offers each day to our Lord Jesus Christ. She has her purpose before her each day, and knows that she wants to live and move with Christ forever.

Sophia's life is an exemplary model of perseverance and endurance. It should be such for us that when we think we have no more strength to go on, to consider those, who like Sophia, are joyful every day of their existence despite having no ability to remedy their own situation. It is here that we need to find our motivation and thanksgiving to God in that He never gives us more than we can handle in our lives. When we offer our suffering, we are doing his Will and making our way to heaven and helping others. Remembering that this is our main purpose on earth, to get past the test and make it to our heavenly home. Jesus said to Saint Faustina, *"You please me most when you meditate on My sorrowful Passion. Join your little sufferings to my sorrowful Passion, so that they may have infinite value before My majesty"* (Michelenko, pg. 203). We love you Sophia, and are most grateful that God gave you to us as an example of sheer strength.

Saint Maximillian Kolbe, Beyond Strength and Courage

For those of you who do not know the story of St. Maximillian Kolbe, may I suggest you read the whole story of his dedication to Jesus through the Blessed Virgin Mary. Again, I cannot provide all the details of his incredible journey, but this powerhouse saint is a model of Victory for Christ over the worst of evil. There is no way to give justice to his story of courage in this brief recap, but I am honored to introduce you to him for further study. What he did in terms of sacrifice and strength makes him one of the greatest saints of the 20th century.

This example is provided to the reader in that sometimes giving of oneself in entirety on the behalf of another will fulfill your purpose in life and demonstrate the love for both God and neighbor. It can bring others to God, and this is part of our mission to Christ. This is surely an example where one finds the reason for life in the giving it away for others. The strength and courage this saint manifested in the direct face of the evil shows the faith and understanding he had of his God, and what opportunity was given him to sacrifice himself in totality. Let us contemplate the life of St. Maximillian Kolbe.

St. Maximillian Kolbe (his birth given name was Raymond) came from a deeply Catholic family firmly founded in tradition and faith. Born in 1894 in Zdunska-Wola Poland, he was one of three brothers whose father was a working man in the midst of much adversity. The family lived in a deeply divided mother country due to the upheaval and unrest of the time. His mother taught him a great deal regarding the Mother of God, the Blessed Virgin Mary, for whom he developed an innermost devotion and love (saintmaximiliankolbe.com). He learned many prayers and quickly grew in grace and wisdom at an early age.

While he was virtuous, Raymond was a natural boy and got into some mischief. He was rambunctious even as his faith life started to influence him. One day his real mother was frustrated at his lively behavior and asked him, "*What will become of you?!*". Raymond was sensitive to his mother's admonishment, and brought the same tearful question to the Blessed Mother in his prayers. (saintmaximiliankolbe.com).

It was reported that the Blessed Mother, allowed a vision to come to Raymond that showed him two crowns, one red, and one white. Raymond was asked then to choose which crown he was to choose. The white one demonstrated a life that would be singular in devotion as a priest and serve Jesus Christ through the Blessed Mother's guidance, and the red crown represented that he could become a martyr for Jesus Christ. Raymond chose both crowns as a true saint would, and both crowns would prove to become true.

His given name of Raymond was changed to "Maximillian Mary", a name he chose after joining the Franciscan order in 1907. Max spent many hours of prayer before the Holy Eucharist. As many souls devoted to Christ, Maximillian endured difficult trials and tribulations as a young growing Franciscan novitiate. He wanted to do great things for God through the Blessed Mother. This included contemplating leaving the Franciscan order for Polish military service, but it was not God's plan for him. (saintmaximiliankolbe.com).

During his studies in Rome, he focused on the Primacy of Jesus Christ. He was a very learned and dedicated student. He determined that to be perfect in love and discipleship for Christ, one had to emulate and learn how to love Christ as the Blessed Virgin Mary loved Christ.

A year before his ordination he founded the Knights of the Immaculate or the Militia Immaculata (M.I). (saintmaximiliankolbe.com). Like so many of the time, Maximillian contracted tuberculosis after he had returned to Poland in 1919. As a young priest, he tried to do many confessions at the time but his condition made him weak. Nonetheless, Maximillian went on to form two larger evangelization sites, one in Poland called the "City of the Immaculata", and the other in Japan. Maximilian was technologically savvy and used short wave radio to expand the program. He even planned on developing a television studio in Poland (https://militiaoftheimmaculata.com).

The City of the Immaculata, formed in 1939, would prove to accept and house many of the Jewish refugees that were fleeing Nazi occupation. In 1941, St. Maximillian was arrested for assisting the Jews and sent to Auschwitz, Poland. This infamous death camp became an extermination tool of extreme proportion for the Nazi regime.

It was here that St. Maximillian gives us one of the most profound selfless examples of the modern era. It was said that after three prisoners escaped from Auschwitz about a month after Fr. Max had arrived, the German officer in charge was very angry and ordered that ten men die by starvation in punishment for the escape (sfi.usc.edu/news). One of the ten chosen was said to be distraught because he had a family and needed to try to support them again one day. He begged the German officer to spare his life. Fr. Max stepped up and offered an astonishing proposal to the German officer.

He requested that he, Fr. Max, substitute his life for the man with the family, and have his sentence conferred upon himself. What kind of thinking was this and why would Fr. Max decide to offer his life in full for this man? The witnesses state that Father Kolbe lasted two weeks from starvation, and outlasted the other nine prisoners.

When the German commandant found that Fr. Max had not died, he was furious and ordered Fr. Max to be killed by lethal injection of carbolic acid (https://sfi.usc.edu/news). It was stated that Fr. Max was in a state of ecstasy and held out his arm as if welcoming the injection that would send him to Jesus (saintmaximiliankolbe.com). This remarkable heroism obviously had an effect on all those who witnessed and lived to tell the story.

Fr. Maximillian Kolbe was declared a saint of the Roman Catholic Church on Oct. 10th, 1982. For there is "*no greater love than this, that a man lays down his life for his friend*" (Jn 15:12). Can this example help you find purpose in life?

When one thinks of all the lives that were tragically ended because of inhumane treatment in these camps, it reminds us of current mistreatments that some undergo in today's society. When humans decide to treat other humans as objects, respect for life ceases to exist. This is similar to the great tragedy of abortion in our world today. We need to find alternatives to killing our innocent little brothers and sisters. God expects us to cherish and respect life.

If I could have the reader take away one thing from the story of St. Maximillian Kolbe it would be the following: One can find consolation and purpose in doing great things of the utmost dignity by confirming the significance of other brothers and sisters. That is exactly what St. Maximillian did.

If you focus your concern on your brother's and sister's needs, God has an abundant gift to give you for your selflessness. That gift is eternal life with Him wearing a crown of honor for all eternity! No one will be able to take this gift from you. Please ponder that thought. Thank you,

Fr. Maximillian, for standing up to evil and being glorified in Christ for your deeds of heroism in rescuing others from death!

The Blessed Virgin Mary's Holy Example

In Lourdes France in 1858, a young maiden Bernadette Soubirous, experienced a visitation in an apparition from our Blessed Mother Mary. This is now a very special place of healing and asking for the Blessed Mother's intercession to Jesus. During this encounter, The Blessed Virgin revealed herself to Bernadette with the words, "I am the Immaculate Conception," thus bestowing Heaven's blessing on the new dogma for the Catholic Faith. (Catholicbridge.com). It was only shortly prior to that time in 1854 that the Church had proclaimed this infallible truth regarding our Blessed Mother being the Immaculate Conception, the Mother of Jesus. This was a remarkable affirmation that Heaven had allowed this truth to be verified in those words to Bernadette.

The Immaculate Conception refers to Mary being born without original sin, as She was chosen by God the Father to be the *new* Ark of the Covenant. She would go on to give Her *"fiat"*, Her *"Yes"* back to God to become Mother of the Savior. She was devoid of sin since birth and throughout Her life. She was spotless from all sin including original sin by the grace of God. This was the only befitting way to carry our Lord Jesus (who is perfect and without sin) in Her womb. Our Lord honored the Blessed Mother with the title *Queen of Heaven* for Her faithfulness.

Saving the most Intimate of examples for last, one has to contemplate the life of the Blessed Virgin Mary, our Holy Mother. It is very difficult, if not impossible to fathom all that God bestowed upon the humble virgin. To be chosen to be the Mother of God, while at the same time being created by God like the rest of us, grants to Her honor, privilege, royalty, and dignity that no other creature can say he or she has been awarded. This did not mean, however, that She would not suffer. On the contrary, one might make a case that the Blessed Mother was second only to Christ in Her overall sacrifice and suffering that She persevered through and endured.

Saving this best example for last, there are too many directions one author could take about Her purpose in the salvation of mankind. Instead, I want to continue with the theme that She, our Holy and Blessed Mother is the Promised Land. That is to say that She, with the fulfillment of Her overall purpose, is leading us into the reign of Her Immaculate Heart and pointing us to Jesus.

This reign simultaneously leads us into the reign of Jesus's Sacred Heart. When a person speaks of reigning, one is speaking about a Kingship and/or Queenship that involves sovereignty. This is exactly the case. Our Queen Mother will usher in the reign of our King and Lord Jesus Christ. With as many apparitions that are taking place in today's world, She is preparing us and pleading with us to make ready our own hearts for Her Son.

Amazingly, this is foretold to us and written about in Holy Scripture. More than several mystics (those who receive a special spiritual ability to interact with Heaven) have both in the recent past (the past 150 years or so), and currently, foretold that, the Blessed Mother, will be the one to pilot in the New Era of Peace. In this way we will live united to Jesus spiritually and physically in a new era of peace.

This Era will not be one in which Jesus comes for final judgement, but one where we can live in peace and prosperity since the world will be purified from all the evil it now knows. Before this can happen, it is also designated that the world must take the side of either Christ who came to save us, or the evil one. This is part of your purpose. You must be ready in your heart to receive Jesus at any time, for one does not know when the "thief" comes. In Matthew 24:43-44 Jesus says, *"But understand this: if the owner of the house had known in what part of the night the thief was coming, he would have stayed awake and would not have let his house be broken into. Therefore, you also must be ready, for the Son of Man is coming at an unexpected hour."*

If we start to contemplate God's plan for salvation, we begin to take into account again all that the Blessed Mother is and will become for mankind. She is the Mother of the Holy Roman Catholic Church and Her Magisterium founded in 33 A.D. She is the mother of mankind in which all humans have a right to Her protection, intercession, and motherly love! While we cannot delve into this in full, one has to understand that She was born without original sin under God the Father's direction. Much like He brought Adam and Eve into the world without original sin so He did for Mary.

She, as the carrier of the God-Man Jesus Christ, was not to be with sin, since He is without sin, then, now, and forever! Once you accept this and understand that She has a role in your life, the graces start to pour over you and they keep coming. She is the Morningstar. She is a way that God has chosen for His people to overcome evil in full through Jesus Christ. Let us consider all the importance that St. Mary Ever Virgin has as an example for us and who shows us purpose.

Consider how supremely special it is to be chosen as the one and only human that will be worthy enough (by God's immense grace), to bring the Son of God, the Second Person in the Trinity, to the world. The story goes that the Blessed Mother's mother, St. Anne, was a very holy woman who would grow up and meet another virtuous man St. Joachim. As Mary's parents, the two lived an austere life. It was a life that put God first. Both knew the importance of making God the ultimate focus of their marriage.

St. Anne and Joachim suffered by not being able to have children for years. Finally, St. Anne conceived after many years of trials, prayers to God, and a testing of their faith. It was said that the promise the couple made to God was that they would dedicate their daughter to God at the age of three, where She would grow up in the temple and live a life dedicated to serving God. This is what occurred and the Blessed Mother found herself in God's care at a very young age.

Mary would occasionally get to see Her parents when they would visit Jerusalem on pilgrimage, but how hard of a suffering it must have been for both child and parents to be separated. This may give courage and comfort to those who have family separation in their lives. Yes! Jesus's maternal grandparents were good and holy people who honored their promise to God. This allowed this young maiden to be pliable in God's Will for the human race.

Mary grew and learned in the temple. She was a hard worker that understood the meaning of difficult labor. Mary grew in perseverance, inner endurance, and strength to serve God. She had previously taken an inner oath to remain a virgin, so you can imagine Her surprise when St. Gabriel said to Her, (while She was only an early teenager), that She would conceive and bear a son by the overshadowing and power of God the Holy Spirit. At this point Mary was betrothed to another very Holy man, St. Joseph, but the two were not intimate.

This must have weighed tremendously on the Blessed Mother's mind as a young and scared teenager, who was not married yet. She did not say "No", but She said "Yes" to one of the most important decisions in all of history. This *"fiat"*, or *"yes"*, to God, was to becoming the Mother of the person who was to reverse original sin. The one who would make it possible for heaven to be open since it was shut from the fall of Adam and Eve. Mary was the one who would bring Salvation Himself into existence.

Mary and Joseph would experience many sorrows and pain, however, with this decisive and crucial *"Yes"* answer, the world changed. Recall that the Blessed Mother, at the time of Jesus's presentation in the temple, (an act of dedicating the child back to God) was told that Her heart would be pierced with a sword . This is because Jesus would endure much suffering. For whatever reason, how many new mothers, (especially young mothers), are subject to hearing something similar?

Then, after Jesus is born, His life is threatened by King Herod the jealous and brutal king of the region who is set to murder any threat to his power that may exist. Mary and Joseph have to flee miles on foot to Egypt, a foreign country, where they know very few individuals. How many of us have to leave and go places we do not want to go, and yet persevere with life until things become stable and calm?

After nine years, the Holy Family leaves Egypt, and return to the town of Nazareth. It is in Nazareth that they live a holy and humble life around certain kinsman of both Mary and Joseph. Joseph has also taken an oath of remaining a virgin to offer to God his singular devotion to both Mary and God. This was a sacrifice to live as brother and sister, and yet love one another for the sake of raising Jesus in holiness.

When Jesus was twelve years of age, the Blessed Mother and Joseph lose Jesus for three days on one of the pilgrimages back to Jerusalem where they had celebrated the Jewish Passover celebration. Consider the anguish, anxiety, and fear that Mary and Joseph experienced in losing the child of God. How each had to be strong and keep looking until their child was found safe in the midst of teaching other adults about God and His Kingdom. Call to mind all parents who have physically lost a child for whatever reason and then are expected to somehow continue to live life in a normal fashion.

I would like to believe there is a special place in heaven where these parents are reunited with a lost child. The pain is unspeakable, the heartbreak inconsolable, and the sadness is one only God can fully appreciate. If you happen to be one of these parents who have lost a child, reach out to our heavenly Blessed Mother. She will console you with the grace that only God can provide through Her. She understands your loss in its entirety. She will help heal the pain.

If these experiences were not bad enough, consider that our Blessed Mother knew all along that Her "*Yes*" to bringing Jesus into the world, would someday end in a most horrific tragedy. The tragedy in which

She would fully rely on God to bring Her through. She knew Jesus would die a very brutal death. However, She did not allow this thought to overcome Her faith in God.

Take a moment to think this reality over. Now take a moment to say "*Thank you God for creating such a loving and strong creature in Mary*", and for providing for us His Mother to be an intercessor for our causes. Finally, say, *"Thank you"*, to Mary for Her holy perseverance.

Mary had to witness Her own child, whom She knew was God's Holy Son, walk the hateful road to His crucifixion on Golgatha. On the way, Jesus fell three separate times under the weight of the cross-beam, was nailed to timbers, and was hoisted in the air only to die hours after hanging by His flesh. It is stated that when Jesus said from the Cross, *"I am thirsty"*, (John 19:28), He said this for His Mother's benefit. He said this because She had provided water and drink for Him as a child, and that She, His Mother, wanted to provide for Him again as a demonstration of their close union as mother and child. It makes one pause, and envelop oneself in the mystery of their close relationship. Jesus and Mary both participated in God's plan of salvation to overcome evil. They united their hearts to fulfill God's will.

Is it any easier after reading this writing and judging the saint's examples to understand that this whole purpose in life is to beat evil, and let your faith and works, namely your strength, perseverance, and endurance be demonstrated to God? When a person collectively and cumulatively offers up all they encounter in life for God, in continuous acts of free will towards God, it is here He finds us worthy of His love. We are worthy for life in heaven forever.

Consider a few last details about our Blessed Mother's virtues. In the Catholic tradition, we try and recall Jesus's passion and crucifixion with a scripturally and traditionally based prayer called the Stations of the Cross. Station number four, of this fourteen-part prayer has one reflect on how strong Our Blessed Mother was when She actually met Jesus on His way to Calvary as described above.

This prayer takes one "station" at a time to reflect and pray regarding what He and She endured. It would take much effort to not do all in one's power to save a loved one from torture. This prayer regarding the stations is mentioned one more time to have the reader exclusively put themselves in Our Blessed Mother's shoes. After knowing She had borne the Savior of the world, and watching the world make the biggest mistake of all time in killing Him, still had to meet Him on His road to the cross. She had to dig deep and muster much strength, and is why She is worthy of our honor.

Richard Furey (*Mary's Way of the Cross* author), has a reflection that might help illustrate Mary's valiant courage and faith in God the Father. He narrates the reflection of Mary at meeting Her son at this junction in His agonizing walk. *"I managed to break through the crowd and was walking by my son. I called to him through the shouting voices. He stopped. Our eyes met, mine full of tears and anguish, his full of pain and confusion. I felt helpless; then his eyes said to me, "Courage!" There is a purpose for this." As he stumbled on, I knew he was right. So, I followed and prayed silently*. (pg. 9, Fourth Station). This quote edifies our entire theme for the book. There is purpose in life and in doing the Will of God. We are to follow Jesus no matter what the cost.

This scene should pivot our minds back to remembering that we have this purpose in life to be strong and follow Jesus. Even through the harshest and cruelest difficulties we are to carry our own cross like Jesus explains. *"If any want to become my followers, let them deny themselves and take up their cross and follow me. For those who want to save their life will lose it, and those who lose their life for my sake will find it"* (Matthew 16 : 24-25). He promises that the purpose is ultimately life with Him in heaven.

Does your mind ever wander when you start thinking of the possibilities in heaven? It is exciting, but St. Paul tells us our intellects and capacities cannot really grasp what we will experience. It is promised to be beyond awesome and something unique each day in eternity if we simply love Him and stick out this test. *'What no eye has seen, nor ear heard, nor the human heart conceived, what God has prepared for those who love him'* (1 Corinthians 2: 9).

To love Him means to do what He says and to pick up your cross each day. It also means though, that your cross may differ in the various seasons of life. Remember, you can ask Jesus to help you carry whatever your cross might be. The cross to Jesus is His Glory as we discussed. He will help us too without question.

Returning to the Virgin Mary's anguish. She did not run and hide when the soldiers hung Jesus on the Cross, but stayed with Him. She held His sacred body in death when Joseph of Arimathea took Him down for burial. She had to wait a heart-rending time like the others for Jesus to be raised from the dead. She no doubt gathered the distraught disciples and apostles while they mourned for Jesus, and were scared for their own lives.

She guided Peter and John and the rest of the apostles until they could experience the strength and courage the Holy Spirit provided at Pentecost. Pentecost is the time when the Holy Spirit came and entered into the apostles 50 days after Christ died. Mary lived many more years in a capacity serving and initiating the Catholic Church. We will not know all She accomplished for us, Her children, in Her last years here on earth before being assumed into heaven. (Tradition teaches us that the Blessed Mother was taken into heaven body and soul at Her Assumption). This is something one can review in more detail by reading the Catechism of the Catholic Church. We all owe our Heavenly mother a huge debt in saving us by bearing us the Savior. Let that sink in. Recall what Mary said in Her Magnificat, *"Surely, from now on all generations will call me blessed, for the Mighty One has done great things for me, and holy is his name."* (Luke 1, 48-49).

CHAPTER THIRTEEN

Draw From His Grace and Light

Are you experiencing any of these examples?

Reflect upon what you can do to remedy your life's issues and call Jesus Christ to help you by drawing on our Lord 's grace and assistance. You can also ask the Father to help you in the name of Jesus. Here is a small prayer you can say often to help you with your situations *"May the Precious Blood of Jesus Christ save us and the whole world!"*

Consider the state of life you are now experiencing. Here are some examples of the need to call on our Lord and Savior Jesus. There is power in His Holy name.

"Jesus please help me!"

- Are you someone in desperate need of breaking the devil's stronghold in your life? *Call to Jesus*
- Are you living a reality in which financial needs are crushing you and your family? *Call to Jesus*
- Are you in an abusive relationship in which love seems to be a one-way street? *Call to Jesus*
- Does the evil of pornography, gambling, computer use or money have you paralyzed? *Call to Jesus*
- Is the life you are living one without a purpose? Do you question the meaning of life? *Call to Jesus*
- Have you caused infidelity in your relationship with your spouse? *Call to Jesus*

- Do you have the temptations to live in a homosexual or transexual relationship, but want to live a life of purity and abstinence and be singular for God? *Call on Jesus.*
- Do you live in a world where you are simply void of God? *Call to Jesus.*
- Are you a teenager or young person that has no direction in life? *Call to Jesus.*
- Are you a parent whose burden is heavy because of the love for a wayward child, a child with a disability, a child who will not show respect, a child that is inappropriately acting out? *Call to Jesus*
- Are you involved with various vices and need to break evil's grip? *Call to Jesus.*
- Are you someone struggling with being a kind, gentle, charitable person? *Call to Jesus.*
- Are you solely focused on yourself and continuously worried only about you? *Call to Jesus*
- Do you perform immoral deeds for services, and have a desire for dark things? *Call on Jesus*
- Do you suffer from medical issues that you did not have prior, but now experience after years of hating or not forgiving someone? *Call to Jesus*
- Do you find yourself doubting the existence of God because others tell you that belief in God is antiquated? *Call to Jesus*
- Are you a person who has spent a good portion of their life in trouble with the law, or someone who has had to endure prison and or jail for long periods, and do not know how to restore relationships and transitioning back to the culture? *Call on Jesus.*
- Are you dangerously dabbling in the occult and new age movement? *Call on Jesus.*
- Maybe you are a person who has had an abortion, or helped someone obtain an abortion, or have committed the act of providing an abortion. It is not too late. *Call on Jesus.*

- Are you someone who has committed sins you do not want to mention, and yet you know deep down they are the reason for your misery and trouble? *Call on Jesus!*
- Are you a religious that has participated in some sins that you now are too embarrassed to bring forth to the priest in confession? You need to hear that it is most definitively not too late to call on our Lord for His magnificent and unfailing mercy. *Call out to Jesus now!*
- Are you at your wits end or believe that your problems are too big for Our Lord? Many people get to this point, and it is because of the evil that constantly bombards us each day. Remember you can call on our Lord. You also have a loving Mother in heaven and She is waiting to introduce Herself to you if you will allow. *Call out to Jesus and His Mother Mary.*

Go through this list and examine your circumstances. Seek Jesus by Calling to Him!

- Are you just to the point in life where you want to give up, not go on another day, and or end your life? Do not give in! This is the evil one, and if you call on the name of Jesus He will come to your aid!
- Are you a person who is overly demanding of others, belittling others, hating with your heart, and someone who cannot find internal peace? Do you cause everyone you come into contact with, or those you love have major turmoil and trouble in their lives? Do your words or actions build up, or tear someone down? Call on Jesus and make a firm amendment of your life to reverse this behavior.
- Do you blame others for your problems instead of taking actions on your own to fix these issues? Call on Jesus to help you take the first steps to reversing this behavior.

- Do you hate authority, or listen to the false news in the media? Pray to Jesus to help know the truth when you hear it, and reject false things.
- Do you wish ill on others rather than pray for them to have God's blessings? Call to Jesus to change this mindset and your heart.
- Do you wish to confess your sins and get them off your soul forever? Time to call to Jesus to show you the pathway to His Holy Church. (It will be the best move of your life guaranteed!)
- Are you a workaholic and someone who is bitter or cannot forgive oneself and would rather not be around people? Call on Jesus to soften the heart, and to give you the rest you need to live a healthier and balanced life.
- Are you someone that needs a miracle, that needs a huge burden lifted from your life? Call on Jesus, He specializes in miracles!
- Maybe you are being forced to follow Islam and are being mistreated, and are looking for a way out? Call on Jesus, He will enlighten you to the truth. He is Truth.
- Are you someone who needed to hear these words to find purpose in life? Call on Jesus to be your Way, your Truth, and your Life.
- Are you someone who wants to help yourself improve and make life less busy, less confusing, less demanding? Call on Jesus to filter out the noise and get rid of things you do not need.
- Are you someone who desires to become more holy, to come closer to our Lord? Call on Jesus through the Blessed Mother's help to lead you to the Catholic Church, the one true Church. Jesus founded this Church for you to receive the sacraments, including His Holy Body and Blood. You will then be on your way to your final dwelling place!
- Finally, if anything at all in this book helped you to become closer to God, please do your part, your mission as we discussed and evangelize someone else by giving them this text to help them! Call out to Jesus to point out to you someone in your life that might need to hear these words!

One place to start calling on our Lord Jesus is to recall what He has first endured for you. Try this prayer as a start for a new relationship with our Lord Jesus Christ.

Prayer In Honor of Jesus's Holy Virtues:

O Lord Jesus Christ, I wish to reverently honor and worship Your Holy virtues of Strength, Perseverance, and Endurance. I wish to acknowledge that you lived 33 years knowing full well that Your purpose was to be born into the darkness of this world, love and teach your people, and provide the opportunity for salvation by suffering torture and death. Your example of these virtues was demonstrated by bearing false accusations and hatred throughout your ministry while doing the Father's Will. You cured physical, mental, and most importantly spiritual needs. Lord Jesus, You did all of this knowing that Your end was one of incredible pain, rejection, and mental anguish. Inspire us not to despair in our own daily struggles Lord and help us continue to fight against the evil one. You persisted in the Garden of Gethsemane despite sweating blood. You sustained betrayal and beatings before your false accusers. You were finally abandoned to a death by crucifixion. All of this you did to fulfill the Father's Will, while promising that if we followed Your "Way of the Cross" that we too would experience eternal life in your resurrection. I pray that You allow the grace of these three virtues of Holy Strength, Perseverance and Endurance be granted to me to follow Your example and fulfill the Father's Will in my life.

Now go and find that purpose in life by following the Way, the Truth, and the Life to get to your heavenly dwelling place in the Father's House. Find that peace you deserve in Jesus Christ. You have the encouragement and where-with-all to get to your dwelling place. It is time this day to get started, do not wait another moment for your own sake! May God bless you!

"*For God has destined us not for wrath, but for obtaining salvation through our Lord Jesus Christ, who died for us, so that whether we are awake or asleep we may live with him.*" (1 Thes. 5: 9-10).

APPENDIX A

Surrender Novena, www.hallow.com/blog/
how-to-pray-the-surrender-novena

H.O.M. Ministries 108 Aberdeen St. Lowell, MA 01850

BIBLIOGRAPHY

References

The Holy Bible, New Revised Standard Version, Catholic Edition, Anglicized Text, Harper Collins, 1995

The Pieta Prayer Booklet, Miraculous Lady of Roses, Hickory Corners, Michigan. 1972

Deliverance Prayers, Fr. Chad Ripperger, Ph.D. Sensus Traditionis Press, 2018

Merriam Webster Dictionary, 2024

The Holy See, St. Augustine of Hippo, Confessions, 1, 1.5, www.vatican.va

The Catechism of the Catholic Church, Double Day, First Book Edition, 1995.

Surrender Prayer, Father Dolindo Ruotolo, Appendix A.

The Holy Ghost Our Greatest Friend, He Who Loves Us Best, Father Paul O'Sullivan O.P. Tan Books and Publishers, Inc. 1952.

Vicky Smith, Healer in the Name of Jesus, Mystic and Author, O Crux Ave Media, You Tube, 2024

WWW. Hallow.com, How-to-Pray-the-Surrender-Novena.

Cale Clarke, Relevant Radio Show Host, Series on Jesus, 101. 2025.

The Wisdom of Fulton Sheen, Matthew Kelly, Blue Sparrow, 2019.

Bibliography

Introduction to the Devout Life, St. Francis De Sales, Doubleday, 1989.

Oxford Languages Dictionary, Copyright 2025 Oxford University

Did We All Come from Adam and Eve, Dr. Elizabeth Mitchell, 2013, The Economist, "All About Adam"

Following the Holy Spirit, Rev. Walter Van De Putte C.S.SP., Catholic Book Publishing Co. New York, NY 1990.

True Devotion to Mary, St. Louis De Monfort, Translated by Fr. Fred Faber, Tan Books and Publishers, 1985.

The Sorrow, The Sacrifice, and the Triumph, Thomas W. Petrisko, Touchstone, New York, NY. 1995.

Thomas More, A Portrait of Courage, Gerard Wegemer, 1998, Scepter Publishing Press

Mercy My Mission, Life of Sister Faustina H. Kowalska, S.M.D.M, Sr. Sophia Michalenko, C.M.G.T, Marian Press, 1987.

In Christ Alone, Keith Getty and Stuart Townsend, Exulthim.org, 2021

https://militiaoftheimmaculata.com, 2025 by Militia of the Immaculata.

saintmaximiliankolbe.com, Biography of St. Maximillan Kolbe.

https://sfi.usc.edu/news/2016/08/12019-religious-resistance-auschwitz-sacrifice-saint-kolbe, Religious Resistance in Auschwitz, Story of Saint Kolbe.

Praying the Stations, Mary's Way of the Cross. Richard Furey, Twenty-Third Publications, 1984.

The Baltimore Catechism of 1891, The Catholic Primer, 2005

The New Saint Joseph Baltimore Catechism, Official Revised Edition, 1964, by Fr. Bennet Kelly, Catholic Book Publishing Co., New York.

Zachary King, Satanist turned Catholic, YouTube -2022

St. Michael and the Angels, Tan Books, Copyright 1977, Tan Books and Publishers, Inc.

Relevant Radio, The Patrick Madrid Show, Patrick Madrid, Oct. 31, 2025.

St. Bernard of Clairvaux, Catholicculture.org

Transitions by the Book, www.Transisitonsbythebook.com, 2025

www.webmd.com, Hemadrosis.

www.Catholicbridge.com, Historical Timeline for the doctrine of the Immaculate Conception. 2025

Wordhippo.com

Catholic Devotions for Men 2026 A Guide to Strength and Faith, Liam A. Brooks, Coppell, Texas December 2025.

www.ingramcontent.com/pod-product-compliance
Lightning Source LLC
LaVergne TN
LVHW010613100826
845148LV00014B/2942

* 9 7 9 8 2 1 8 9 4 7 8 2 8 *